D0848794

A BEAUTIFUL
PINT

A BEAUTIFUL PINT

IAN RYAN

One man's search
for the perfect
pint of Guinness

BLOOMSBURY PUBLISHING
NEW YORK • LONDON • OXFORD • NEW DELHI • SYDNEY

BLOOMSBURY PUBLISHING
Bloomsbury Publishing Inc.
1385 Broadway, New York, NY 10018, USA

First published in Great Britain 2023
First published in the United States 2024

ISBN: HB: 978-1-63973-435-1; eBook: 978-1-63973-436-8

Library of Congress Cataloging-in-Publication Data is available

2 4 6 8 10 9 7 5 3 1

Commissioning Editor: Grace Paul
Project Editor: Faye Robinson
Typeset by Ed Pickford
Design by Vaughan Mossop

Printed and bound in Great Britain by
CPI Group (UK) Ltd, Croydon CR0 4YY

For Mary, Noel, Lisa, Rebecca, Peggy

and all the lads who drank

with me along the way

CONTENTS

Shtick/stick

Lacing on a pint

Dome/domeage

A domed
head on a
pint

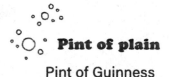

Pint of plain

Pint of Guinness

GUINNESS

The black stuff

Guinness

The tilt test

When you tilt a pint
slightly sideways
and the creamy head
shows itself

Guinness game/ splitting the G

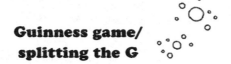

Drinking down to the G on the
Guinness logo on the glass
within first sup of a pint

GLOSSARY

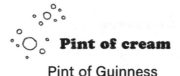

Pint of cream

Pint of Guinness

Guiness and Black

Pint of Guinness with
blackcurrant cordial
(heathen behaviour)

Introduction

What is it that makes Guinness so special, so recognisable, so beloved? So much so that a quarter of a million people will follow an Instagram account about badly poured pints of it? This book is an attempt at answering these questions.

I'll talk about my own relationship with Guinness, give a brief overview of its history and describe how the iconic drink we all know today came to be. I'll touch on its most iconic adverts over the years and its impact on modern culture, including some of my experiences running Guinness-based social media accounts, like the time I received a threatening message from a pub landlord in the middle of the night, and when I poured an awful pint on morning television. With that humiliation behind me, I'll investigate the different factors that can make it a Beautiful Pint or a Shit London Guinness.

Finally, and most usefully, I'll take a look at some of the best pubs around the world to drink Guinness in. See you up at the bar sometime...

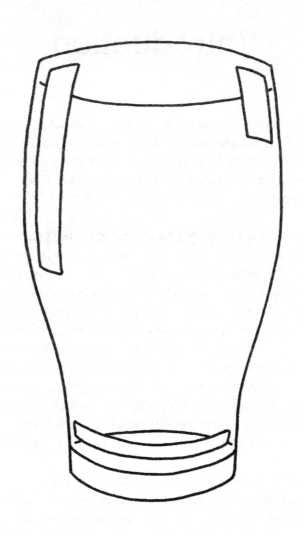

1.

Guinness & Me

THE YEARS BG
(BEFORE GUINNESS)

I was never a Guinness drinker until I left Ireland.
Strange, I know, considering how five years later I
have ended up as some sort of pseudo-authority on
the subject – and writing this book about it – but
I just never considered it something that a young
person would drink.

When we were young lads in Cork, we all drank
cheap vodka, cheap lager, cheap cider – not
always in that order, but sometimes, and not
always at once, but sometimes. Resources were
scarce in post-recession Ireland and, like lads

being rescued from an ill-prepared excursion across the Sahara, you drank what you could get your hands on. We played a horrendous game called King's (which has a bunch of other apt names, like King's Cup, Circle of Death, Ring of Fire), where eventually you had to down the big communal cup full of the various kinds of alcohol people had been pouring into it while playing. Grim. We played another game called Pyramids, which I won't go into, but let's just say a friend blames me for the scar above his eyebrow to this day. Sorry, Jack.

We never spent a lot of time in pubs as young fellas. We probably had €20 for a night out, which was used carefully and tactically to ensure we would be able to get drunk before the club through pre-drinks, with enough booze spare to stash in our pockets in small vodka bottles that would sneakily be deposited into glasses of mixer throughout the night. There was no room in that budget for premium pints of well-poured, well-stored and well-looked-after beers: give me a can of filth instead. One of my best friends, James, and I would always try and hold back a fiver so we could split the cab fare home after the club, but we would inevitably spend it at our favourite local kebab shop, and stumble the forty-five minutes home instead. Happy days.

But, no – Guinness wasn't really a thing for my group of friends growing up. It always felt like something sacred, reserved for only the most powerful of old pintmen, those whose stools had grooves as deep as the mines of Moria and liked to drink in company, but not *with* the company. You  should be able to discern what that means or you may have picked up the wrong book. Something that was drunk by real adult men, not young fellas. A pint to be held in hands that bore the marks of a day's work and the wrinkles of wisdom.

To me, as a young fella, Guinness represented the old Ireland. It was the symbol of what I thought of the country – an old, tired warrior that has braved the test of time and stood tall. A country with character and legacy; ever-present in popular culture, whether you were looking out for it or not. Ireland was enjoyed around the world and so was Guinness. Looking back, that is definitely what drew me to the drink after I'd left home.

MOVING TO THE UK

I first started drinking Guinness shortly after I moved to the UK. I was around twenty-two, and, by then, many of the lads back home had started to be drawn to the pint of plain; it was becoming the norm amongst the group. I had, of course, tried Guinness before moving over. My earliest memory was being given 'a taste' of it at a young age while sitting around a table of uncles at a family gathering. I'm sure some are reading that sentence with horror but sure, look, that was the way of it.

Maybe I was intrigued enough by it to try it again, but realistically I think I was just homesick. I'd moved over abruptly, at three weeks' notice, to live in a strange, chaotic warehouse with over twenty people in deep north London. I'd never once lived out of home and it showed. I spent four months in that warehouse before I moved out, but I reckon I could fill a book with stories about that place alone.

My first pint of Guinness in the UK was in a pub called the Park Tavern, in Finsbury Park. It's very much a mixture of an 'old-school boozer' and an Irish pub, sitting on an unassuming side-street off Stroud Green Road. The couple that run the place are an older Irish couple and the clientele are mainly men in their fifties and sixties, watching a variety of sports on a variety of screens with horse-racing pullouts from the red tops strewn across their tables. My kind of place. One of my best friends and one of the kindest people to ever walk this earth, Ben, was the first of the lads from back home to come visit and we sank many a pint in the smoking area of that pub. My favourite part of bringing new people there is the fact that you need to walk through one of the bathrooms to get to the smoking area – the look on their face when you open the door that says 'smoking area' and someone is stood there washing their hands is always priceless.

My favourite part of bringing new people there is the fact that you need to walk through one of the bathrooms to get to the smoking area – the look on their face when you open the door that says 'smoking area' and someone is stood there washing their hands is always priceless.

I was the first of the lads to emigrate but sadly
not the last. We've ended up all over – Dublin,
Beijing, London and Glasgow seem to be the
main destinations. The Irish are everywhere
and that is probably where a lot of the worldwide
appreciation for Shit London Guinness has
come from: I see it not only in the audience
demographics of the account, but in the fact that
orders for the account's merchandise come from
all over the world. Lads named Patrick living in
Australia and lasses called Ciara having to deal
with her name being pronounced 'kee-a-rah' in
Liverpool. I'll always remember an English friend
of mind telling me about the candidate named
'kee-ah-rah' he interviewed for a role at his
company and I still laugh when I think about it to
this day. Poor Ciara. The appreciation for pints of
Guinness is something we all share – whether you
drink it or not, the sight of a bad pint of Guinness
evokes something inside all of us that makes it a
shared experience. A sense of nationalistic horror.
The knowledge that you're in some dark place, far
from home.

Seeing that kind of thing once I'd got to London
must have planted the seed of Shit London
Guinness (and its more positive counterpart) in
my mind, but it's hard to talk about the ideation,
and formation of the accounts, without talking
about my time on the internet before them. I was

always fascinated with the internet and what people created on it when I was growing up, and I always wanted to get involved. My earliest ventures included uploading lots of pirated Garth Brooks to YouTube, and rickrolling a lot of people. I also had a short-lived *Yu-Gi-Oh* channel, a *Big Bang Theory* meme Tumblr account (shameful) and another channel where I made World of Warcraft music videos using the in-game characters...

My first actual successful endeavour online kicked off in 2015 with the formation of the Humans of The Sesh Facebook account that a friend and I ran. It was a parody of Humans of New York, a massively popular account that posts street portraits of people alongside a story about them – usually heartwarming, touching and genuine. We would take the photos they used and post them with our own made-up stories, usually involving some combination of being a drunken mess, drugs and general muck talk. Many years on, I am very sorry to those people. It became bigger and bigger as we added memes and user-submitted videos to the content, growing to over half a million likes (which was the style at the time). We did a lot of great things with that account before winding it down in 2019: we worked with *VICE* and The Loop, a UK drug-testing organisation that operates at festivals and the like, on a drug harm reduction campaign, organised club nights around the UK and Ireland, DJ'd at festivals and were interviewed by all sorts of media outlets. They were happy auld days.

THE RISE OF SHIT LONDON GUINNESS

And so, one fateful day in November 2019, after Humans of The Sesh had wound down, I created the Shit London Guinness Instagram account with a big hungover head on me. I'd been posting all the bad pints of Guinness I'd been getting in London in a Twitter thread on my personal account for a couple of months, and the lads back home were getting a great kick out of my misery as they sipped their pristine pints of plain. I've always loved a niche account and had been a big fan of the OG Guinness rating accounts like @pintsofplain and @guinnessadvisor, who would regularly give pubs scores out of ten based on their pint. I thought that people might get a kick out of my Shit London Guinness experiences and created the account, certainly not expecting it to gain over 240,000 followers or for me to end up writing this book in the dark corner of one of my locals, as the men sat on stools at the bar wondered what that prick was doing on his MacBook.

I was well positioned in that I already had an established following through Humans of The Sesh and my own personal accounts, so I was able to direct people to look at my collection of shit pints. That, combined with a couple of interviews about the account in the media, helped it grow fairly rapidly, ending up with just over 10,000 followers in under a week. A sister Twitter account (@shitlondonguinn) was set up and it went from there, continuing to grow and receiving more and more user submissions.

Pints I've drunk myself are few and far between on the account these days as I know the spots for a good pint and I generally think the quality of

pints in London has improved over the years. Pints that are sent in by followers are the lifeblood of the account and got me through the coronavirus lockdowns in 2020/21, when I somehow managed to keep the account on a steady growth even though pints weren't being poured, and the tap nozzles had grown dry and lifeless, like an old toy thrown into a cupboard in your bedroom when you start growing hair in your armpits and thinking girls aren't so bad after all. Beautiful Pints (@beautifulpints) was set up as a sister account in December 2020 (on Christmas Day for some deranged reason) to showcase the loveliest pints from all round the world and highlight which pubs people should visit to get a great pint. It's very much the Yin to Shit London Guinness's Yang, and is a great palate cleanser for when you've witnessed one of the horrors that London has to offer.

The Shit London Guinness account has received some criticism in the past for calling out pubs by name. It's hard to do anything online without getting some kind of stick, but Shit London Guinness isn't meant to be a negative account. When a pub is posted, it's not a call to boycott the pub forever or to requisition its Guinness kegs to a better landlord: it is a genuine opportunity for the pub to sort out its act, as they are obviously not serving a quality product. Guinness's quality team now monitors the account and visits every pub posted within a couple of days. This isn't a sort of telling-off situation – I was never the student in a classroom who reminds a teacher there's homework due – but a helping-out one. The Guinness team cleans their taps, provides them with some glassware and makes sure they're pouring good pints before they leave: they even get a little plaque that says they've passed the quality control test. Happy days. Of course, this doesn't mean that they end up sticking to pouring good pints – there are plenty of multiple offenders on the account, but at least we tried.

I've had a fair number of celebrity interactions along the way, with people like Niall Horan (who my little cousin wants me to DM asking him to follow her) interacting with the account and mentioning it in interviews. The biggest mention was when Jamie Dornan was being interviewed on the *Graham Norton Show* for the New Year's Eve 2020 special. He and Emily Blunt were reviewing footage of her poor attempt at pouring a pint in a local pub while filming *Wild Mountain Thyme* in Mayo. Laughing, Dornan said: 'There's an Instagram account called Shit London Guinness. Some legend, I think he's from Cork or something, and basically people send him these awful pints, notoriously awful Guinness, here in London. It's like no head at all, loads of head, sometimes a pint of Guinness in a Heineken glass – just sacrilege. That would be straight on there.' I gained a lot of followers that night, as you can imagine. I DM'd Jamie to offer to send him some merchandise after that and he replied with a selfie of him wearing some already. What a man.

Shit London Guinness has given me so many opportunities and I'm very grateful for all the support shown to my accounts over the years. I've raised over £5,000 for charities, worked directly with Guinness on multiple campaigns and been interviewed by most of the major media publications. I also sell a bunch of merchandise online, which is a side of the business I really enjoy. It's been great working with various artists to design T-shirts and seeing people walking around wearing my clothes always makes me happy.

I'm also quite proud of not just showing people shit pints but steering them towards good pubs. I love getting positive feedback from people about how much they loved a pub I recommended, how it's now their local and so on, and I especially love going to visit one of my favourite pubs after posting about it and having the landlord thank me profusely for driving business towards them. Good pubs – pubs which care for their patrons, their staff and their Guinness – should be rewarded, and the stinkers that couldn't care less about their customers as long as they shell out £22 for a pint of muck and some microwave fish and chips should get in the bin. At its core, Shit London Guinness and Beautiful Pints are about improving the quality of pints and making sure customers get a quality product.

It's famously hard for Irish people to show pride: we are a humble people, bragging or showing off is seen as shameful stuff, but I'm going to blow my own trumpet here and say that Shit London Guinness has helped improve the quality of Guinness in the city. I often hear of people who, when complimenting a pub on its pint, get told that 'they don't want to end up on that Instagram account'. I've definitely seen the quality of pints improve across the city as it has got more popular – asking for a Guinness in an unknown pub in London used to be unnerving, not knowing what ethereal horror would emerge from the taps, but now it's usually pretty decent. Cthulhu, begone. The shadow of Shit London Guinness looms large over the City of London. It's a silent guardian, a watchful protector. A dark pint.

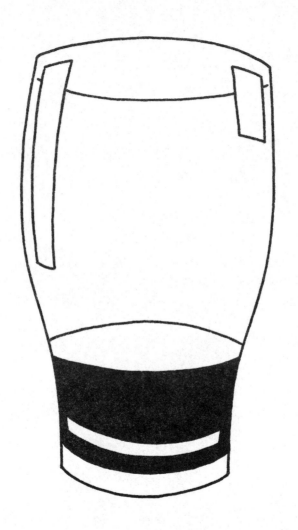

2.

A History of Guinness

STRAIGHT OUTTA KILDARE

Beer has been around for ages. Lads were supping away as far back as Mesopotamia and Ancient Egypt – even the people building the pyramids were allowed a pint a day as part of their rations (indeed, the thick beer brewed back then was an important source of nutrition for the labourers and has been referred to as 'liquid bread'). It has grown, diversified, become a part of cultural, religious and economic movements, and was banned in a few places there for a while, which was bad craic I'd say.

But where did Guinness, specifically, come from? How did it become so popular that some lad from Cork is writing a book about it and going on about the pyramids? Let's have a look.

It all starts with Arthur Guinness. Born in Kildare, of which he is probably the most famous export (not hard, to be fair, it is Kildare), in 1725, Arthur spent his teenage years working in his stepmother's pub and eventually founded his first brewery just outside Dublin in Leixlip, likely inspired by his father, who, as the steward of an estate, had supervised brewing beer for the workers there. Arthur was always passionate about brewing and the innovation alongside it: four years after establishing that first brewery, he moved his operation into Dublin proper, signing the iconic lease for what is now St James's Gate Brewery, which famously lasts for 9,000 years. You can actually see the original lease in the Guinness Storehouse today. This set the foundation for what would become one of the most successful beer companies in history. It saw its initial success brewing ale but in 1778 introduced a porter, the earliest form of which would become Guinness Stout.

Porter itself was a working-class drink favoured among (surprisingly, considering its name) port workers. First brewed in London in the 1700s, it is a dark beer which is nourishing but was still cheap to produce at the time. Within a decade, Guinness's porter had become so popular that he stopped brewing anything else. In 1801, they introduced West India Porter for export to the Caribbean: it's still around, though rebranded as Foreign Extra Stout, a drink my friends and I love. It's now the longest continually brewed recipe in its history and is massive in Asia, Africa and, to this day, the Caribbean. This success and continued innovation led to Guinness being the largest brewery in the world by 1880.

ON TOP OF THE WORLD

By the beginning of the twentieth century, Guinness had gained a reputation as a brewery dedicated to quality and consistency, having implemented rigorous quality control measures and established a dedicated lab for research and testing. It had gained popularity in the UK, Africa, the Caribbean and America. It was also seen as a great employer, providing progressive welfare programmes for employees, housing, healthcare and other benefits. Employees were also entitled to two pints a day for free. Not far off the Egyptians, so, but I'm not really sure the lads who built the pyramids got any pension off the pharaohs.

The 'standard', most popular iteration of Guinness, Guinness Draught Stout, did not come into play until 1959. Where was it hiding until then? Until the mid-twentieth century, Guinness came out of two barrels. I touch on this a bit later in more detail, but basically, one barrel was set to pour foam and the other was for the beer, so pouring a pint was a bit of a balancing act, more of a ritual than it is today. I'm sure somewhere out there in the big wide world, a lager drinker is rolling their eyes, subconsciously sensing someone talking about anything other than firing a pint directly into the glass.

Anyway, there was so much hullabaloo surrounding the pouring, with each bartender seemingly going rogue and having their own

I'm sure somewhere
out there in the big wide
world, a lager drinker
is rolling their eyes,
subconsciously sensing
someone talking about
anything other than
firing a pint directly
into the glass.

system – a bit like pouring a logo on the foam these days, which I think is a mortal sin (unless it's a pentagram, like the one I got from a pub in Canterbury (see p. 127), which was kind of cool). Guinness wanted the pint to have a better and more consistent texture and quality standard, so they needed to streamline the process. Michael Ash, a renowned scientist and mathematician, joined Guinness and came up with his great innovation – adding nitrogen to Guinness. This innovation, which naturally produced a rich foam on the beer, replaced the old taps and

paved the way for Guinness Draught, the drink we know and love today. It was initially named the 'easy serve system', which sounds a bit like something that produces ice-cream; ironically enough, that's what some might call a bad pint of Guinness with too much head these days.

GUINNESS INNOVATIONS

The company has continued to hold innovation at its core and to this day, it is a key to its success. Some of the major innovations since Guinness Draught have been:

THE WIDGET

Have you ever had a can of Guinness at home and wondered what in the world the little plastic ball rattling around in it is? It's a little nitrogen-filled ball called the Widget which helps create that surge in a Guinness, giving it its smooth and creamy texture. It makes drinking cans at home a lovely experience. After its 1988 introduction to market, a survey in the early 2000s voted it as a better invention than the internet, but I'm not sure that would fly these days. Have you ever experienced the joy of receiving an angry message from someone when you beat them on FIFA online? That would get my vote every time. But the Widget is still good.

SURGER CANS

Surger cans were introduced in the mid-2000s, marketed as a new way to enjoy pub-quality Guinness Draught at home. While the Widget used a nitrogen ball to create the surge effect, the surger cans incorporated an electronic surge unit, sold in conjunction with the cans, to recreate the creamy head and cascading effect of a Guinness on tap. They were available for a relatively short period of time for the home market, but were discontinued after a two-year trial. You would still see them in use, albeit rarely, in restaurants or bars that would not be able to sell enough Guinness to justify buying kegs but still wanted to offer it with a slightly more premium option than the can.

However, when the coronavirus lockdowns kicked in, these cans were suddenly in high demand for people at home. The surger cans were still available for purchase from some retailers, but the units to use them with were as rare as a Cavan man buying a round in the pub. There

**It is brewed in
over fifty countries
and over 10 million
glasses of Guinness are
consumed every day
worldwide.**

was much discussion in the Guinness online community about the 'best' way to enjoy a pint from a can while the pubs were unavailable – I even created my own video showing how I believe a Widget can should be poured, which differs slightly from the official method (I think you're better off just tipping it over and pulling the can up as your pour). This led to an innovation of sorts, as people realised you could use an electric jewellery cleaner to recreate the effect of the surge unit, and this then created a shortage of jewellery cleaners available on Amazon. Failing that, some entrepreneurial souls set up kegs in the back of their vans and would drive around to people's houses, parking up outside and pouring fresh pints of Draught Guinness. They were truly wild times. This all became redundant when the below was introduced...

THE NITROSURGE

This has been the most impressive innovation that I've seen in my lifetime as a Guinness drinker. Introduced in September 2021, it is another example of Guinness as a leader in technological innovation – a device that simply clips over a special Nitrosurge can, allowing you to recreate that oh-so-special two-part pour and giving you a beautiful, great-tasting pint from

home. It completely changed the game in my eyes and really delivers, especially for its relatively low price point. I was lucky enough to work with Guinness to unveil the Nitrosurge's release date in the UK and it's always a great present to give, though I wouldn't recommend bringing it as a secret Santa gift to a Christmas party for a job you haven't started yet. The person who got the Nitrosurge realised it came from me and proceeded to try to pour Guinness directly through the device into everyone's mouths in a very, very packed and loud bar at Christmas time. It was a stressful experience as I felt like we'd all get kicked out the door and I'd be told not to bother starting. I'd recommend it as a present for all other occasions, though.

GUINNESS 0.0

I believe everyone was slightly sceptical when Guinness announced a zero-alcohol product and launched it in August 2021. I'd tried plenty of zero-alcohol alternatives to other drinks and they never really did it for me, and that was for other drinks – how could a drink as complex as a Guinness be replicated with zero alcohol while keeping its unique taste? In fact, it actually tastes great – especially on draught. I always have a few lying around in the fridge for an evening where I fancy a pint but don't want to drink. I also helped Guinness with their launch of 0.0, participating in a great livestream with Global Head of Quality, Steve Gilsenan, who is an absolute gent and was able to teach me so much about the product.

It can be easy for me, an Irishman living in the UK, to only speak about Guinness in the context of these countries. However, it's important to remember and recognise how much of a global phenomenon the brand is around the world. It is brewed in over fifty countries and over 10 million glasses of Guinness are consumed every day worldwide. Guinness has continued to go from strength to strength, making strides in quality and consistency, global expansion and marketing. It is one of the most successful and possibly the most iconic beer brands in the world today, its black-and-white pint being as recognis-able as the Golden Arches of McDonalds or Nike's tick. And a large part of that success has come, of course, from advertising.

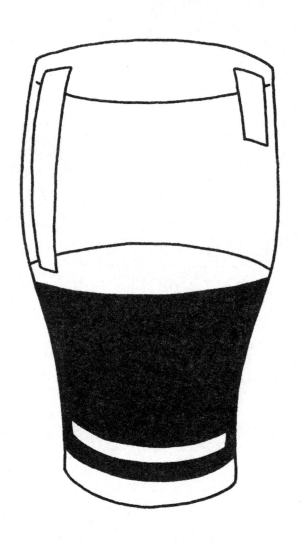

3.

Guinness Culture

ADVERTISING IS GOOD FOR YOU(R BUSINESS)

Guinness has been the king of advertising for over a hundred years. You can probably think of several Guinness adverts right now off the top of your head – how many companies can you say that about? No other drink has such a cult following, with people so passionate about the product that they create online fan accounts with hundreds of thousands of followers, or tattoo symbols of the drink on their bodies. An integral part of how they have achieved this level of loyalty is through their advertising.

The first major Guinness advert was the legendary 1930s 'Guinness is Good for You' campaign, devised by ad agency Benson's. It's said that the 'Guinness is Good for You' line was conceived by legendary crime writer Dorothy L. Sayers, who was a copywriter at the agency at the time. The medical angle was actually plausible way back then, because some doctors ordered new mothers to sup a pint of plain following childbirth so they could get some iron into them. You wouldn't get that these days – advertising regulations have gone soft. They then had 'Guinness for Strength', depicting images of big strong men carrying big

heavy things, presumably doing so after all the pints they were putting away over the weekend gave them big muscles like Popeye with his can of spinach.

The lovely zoo animals were also introduced in the 1930s, with slogans like 'My goodness, my Guinness' accompanying drawings of a sea lion, a little turtle geezer and a toucan; the latter stuck and is one of the most recognisable images of the brand to this day, and something at least two of my close friends have tattooed on their legs. By introducing memorable characters, they were able to add a playful element to the advertising and leave a lasting impression on drinkers' minds. One of my favourite tweets of all time is from @TVsCarlkinsella, which says 'They need to bring back the era of Guinness advertising that was like "drink Guinness with me, the crab."' The slogans were catchy, memorable and helped reinforce the brand recognition.

Guinness has also shone in television advertising, with its first ad on the medium debuting in 1955. Its TV ads have gone from strength to strength over the years, picking up prestigious awards like the Gold Lion at Cannes. I think everyone has one particular ad that stands out to them, depending on their age and location, but for me it is definitely the Christmas advert which shows St

James's Gate with a layer of snow on top, making it look like a pint. This is an idea they'd return to again and again, most recently with their 'Looks Like Guinness' and 'Welcome Back' campaigns, which highlighted various objects that look like pints – black bins with snowy tops, bollards painted black with white heads and black chimneys with seagulls sat on them. Others will remember the 'Surfer' ad from 1998 (the one with the horses), the big man Tom Crean ad from 2002 (the one with the frozen Kerryman), or 'Quarrel' from 2005 (the one with a soaking wet Michael Fassbender).

While they are no longer officially linked, *The Guinness Book of World Records* is surely another reason why Guinness is one of the most recognised brands in the world. Created back in the 1950s after Sir Hugh Beaver, the then managing director of Guinness, had been unable to settle a pub debate around which bird is the fastest, the book collects and celebrates, well, world records – anything from extreme human achievements, like the longest fingernails in the world, to natural phenomena, like the world's oldest cat. It is one of the best-selling books in the world. The sight of a copy always gives me a huge blast of nostalgia – they were the bread and butter of any household when I was growing up in the noughties. I see it a bit like the TikTok of that

The medical angle was actually plausible way back then, because some doctors ordered new mothers to sup a pint of plain following childbirth so they could get some iron into them. You wouldn't get that these days – advertising regulations have gone soft.

time: ten minutes of flipping through records of the tallest men or the world's largest nose gave us precious dopamine hits that are now achieved through the endless scroll.

Guinness has, in this brave new world, also mastered advertising on social media. It has embraced influencer marketing, working with influencers like... well, me. I've been able to help with the launch of some of their more recent products, and was even in their St Patrick's Day social media video advert with Laura Whitmore, though they did Mike Wazowski me in the final edit. No hard feelings.

Its advertising has been so effective that forty, fifty, sixty years on, you still see it on display without them actually having paid for it. Step into any Irish pub the world over and you will see old Guinness advertisements plastering the walls. In the fifty-foot walk from the door to the bar, you might pass four different Guinness signs on the wall, a glass mirror with 'Guinness' inscribed on it, an old man sat up at the bar drinking a fresh, beautiful-looking pint, and when you look up at the bar person, there is a Guinness clock behind them and their hand rests on the iconic harp tap. What are you going to order, a lager shandy? No chance.

GUINNESS AND IRELAND GO TOGETHER LIKE...

A big part of the Guinness brand identity is that strong connection to Ireland. It is seen as Ireland's national drink and one of its national symbols – many associating Guinness with Ireland and vice versa. It has certainly leaned into that connection throughout its history, adopting Brian Boru's harp, a medieval musical instrument on display in Trinity College that also appears on the Irish coat of arms, as its brand logo. Guinness's harp differs slightly, of course – it faces the other way, notably – and has actually changed throughout the years, losing strings as it went, but has now remained unchanged since 2005.

It is, of course, also massively associated with Ireland's national holiday – St Patrick's Day. Guinness is drunk all the world over on 17 March, with some heathens dying it the same green they also dye their rivers on the day, for some reason. Guinness has always invested heavily in its marketing, with their latest 2023 campaign promoting their new zero-alcohol alternative, Guinness 0.0, giving away over 50,000 pints across Ireland on the day, while cleverly encouraging people to 'Make it a St Patrick's Day to remember.'

Sports and cultural event partnerships are an important part of Guinness's marketing and, in Ireland, emphasise the association between the two. In Ireland, they sponsor local community initiatives and music festivals, including Ireland's biggest music festival, Electric Picnic. It has been the title sponsor of the rugby Six Nations Championship since 2019, furthering the brand's connection with Irish culture and sport.

Guinness has also leaned into tourist culture. It's already a tourist activity of sorts: for people visiting Ireland, one of the number one things to do is to go to a pub and drink Guinness. It's an incredible thing when you take a step back and think about it – no one travels to a different country to drink Fosters (at least, I hope not).

As an Irishman living abroad, the first thing I'm asked anytime someone in the office is visiting Dublin is: you're from there, where can I find the best pint of Guinness? First of all, I'm from Cork, so write that one down. But fine, here's a list (for the actual list, see later on in this very book). All of this was happening well before I became the 'Shit London Guinness fella', too. Sit in any Dublin pub during the day and you will hear them make the pilgrimage, accents of all sorts ordering Guinness, but the standout being Americans who have a family connection to

Ireland in some shape or form. They'll look you dead in the eye and tell you they're Irish, while the last Irishman in their family sailed away 180 years ago. We find it endearing, really. For the most part.

The Guinness Storehouse opening as a tourist attraction in 2000 was a stroke of marketing genius. For a lot of tourists, Dublin is a pint-based pseudo-Disneyland already, so what better idea than to create their own version of the Cinderella castle? It has become not just Dublin's top tourist attraction, but the most visited attraction in the whole country, bringing in millions of visitors and functioning basically as one gigantic marketing tool (as well as being genuinely excellent and well worth a visit). The Storehouse gives visitors an immersive experience, letting them learn all about the history of the drink, the brewing processes and that kind of thing. The view from the Gravity Bar is spectacular, to be fair – people can get a bird's-eye view of Dublin and see all of the many pubs they can relax in by purchasing some Guinness after a long afternoon in Guinness Land. One of the main attractions is that visitors get to learn how to pour their own pint, and can even use that strange device that prints pictures onto the head of a pint. That has freaked me out ever since I got a DM on Twitter from an account with no followers that was just a photo of them having used the device to print my face on a pint. Please don't drink me.

Influencers and fan accounts are another string to Guinness's bow (harp) that have cropped up in the last ten years, as you can see from the process that led to this very book. Even though I run one myself, I still find the thought of huge accounts that are dedicated to what is essentially just a product wild. Guinness has done such a good job of creating brand loyalty, and that, combined with its focus on quality, is what I believe led to the rise in these accounts looking to highlight and showcase the pubs that are serving their favourite drink correctly, and, like myself, calling out pubs that are doing it a disservice. These accounts have provided Guinness with what I would imagine is a huge boost – people want to order Guinness so they can share their bad pints with the bad pint accounts, good pints with the good pints accounts, and so on: to have the chance to be featured. As a result, Guinness has created a cottage industry which surrounds it – I have a small business for my account, but other Guinness-focused creators like The Guinness Guru are now full-time content creators, and I'm sure more and more will join him as the years go by.

But when all the marketing's said and done, there's still the real thing: the drink. What *does* make for a good pint of plain?

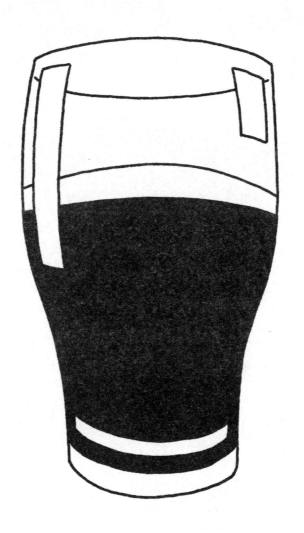

4.

The Pint & The Pour

THE PINT

I am constantly asked what makes a pint of Guinness 'good'. How, people wonder, can a mass-produced drink differ in taste from one pub to the next? In London, for example, you could have five pubs on any given street. Each of these pubs gets the same barrels of Guinness off the same delivery truck. There is no difference in the product they receive, so how can one pub be considered to have a great pint of Guinness and be lauded on social media as a bastion of Guinness quality, while the pub a hundred metres down the road get roasted on Shit London Guinness for pouring an abomination of a pint into a Fosters glass?

It's all about how much they care about it, and the general standard of how their beer is kept. Pubs with poor beer health, only rarely cleaning their lines and giving their glassware sub-par washes, will be able to get away with serving lagers and the like, but will suffer when it comes to their Guinness. Let's start with what makes a pint bad, and then look at what can be done to make it good.

WHAT MAKES A
BAD PINT

☐ Dirty Beer Lines

☐ Big Head

☐ Little Head (Cardboard Box?)

☐ Bubbles

☐ The Wrong Glass

☐ Dirty Glasses

DIRTY BEER LINES

Have you ever tasted a pint and, expecting a creamy, delicious sup, were met with the flavour of a pocket full of coins? I'm not quite sure where I've managed to learn what a pocket full of coins tastes like, I must have enjoyed cracking into a nice handful of pennies as a child, but that bitter, biting taste is the only way I can describe it. It's what happens when a pub's Guinness lines – the pipes running from the keg to the tap – are not washed regularly enough. Beer lines generally need to be washed once a week to avoid a buildup of bacteria and yeast, as well as a bunch of other factors that contribute to the bitter taste that can be associated with poor line cleanliness. I've heard that, given its more complex flavour, Guinness lines should be cleaned a bit more regularly than most, but at the end of the day, I'm just some fella off the internet, so I can't pretend I'm a pub landlord who's been down in the trenches cleaning lines every day. I can only go off what I've learned in my years being 'that Guinness fella'. So: clean your lines.

BIG HEAD

Irish people are naturally predisposed to have large heads: this is a source of national pride and something that makes us easy to spot abroad. I've often found myself in foreign countries, walking on busy streets, and pointing out people who I just know are Irish based on the size of their noggins. It's one of my favourite pastimes – there's no joy like picking out a fella who you can feel in your bones is named Liam and encountering a whisper of a Leitrim accent as he passes by, confirming your suspicions of Irishness.

Large heads on pints, however, aren't something that you want – you don't want to be half-drowning by the time you battle through the head, your nostrils engulfed in a foamy sea, and manage to drink any liquid. It's an offence I see far too often – pints almost reaching a half-head, half-liquid ratio, drawing comments on whether the patron that ordered it had paid for a half pint, or if the bartender had been trying to pour a full.

A lot of the issues come from the wrong gas settings, but other factors like the pour or incorrect glassware can also cause the same problem. Guinness gas settings should be at 70 per cent nitrogen, which gives it its creamy head, and 30 per cent CO_2. Having different settings levels can throw off the pint, giving you too much (or too little) head.

LITTLE HEAD (CARDBOARD BOX?)

It's hard to decide which is worse: too much head or none at all. Drinking a headless pint of Guinness is a joyless experience. Like a cup of tea without milk, a 99 without a flake, or a nostalgic trip to your childhood funfair – it's a similar experience but the fun is negligible. At least, equipped with an oar and steely determination, you can traverse a pint with a large head. With a tiny-headed Guinness, you are left simply to consume the liquid and miss out on the full package. The stout moustache, the telltale sign of a pint well enjoyed, cannot exist in a land of small-headed pints and meagre heads. Pubs – sort out your gas.

BUBBLES

The bubbles! One of the most popular clips I've ever posted was of my friend's Cork father reacting live to the pints on my account. It makes me laugh no matter how much I've watched it, but his best response was to a pint full of bubbles, exclaiming 'the bubbles!' in a thick Cork accent. People still reference this when I post a bubble-heavy pint, and I'd recommend anyone reading this book to pause and look for it on the account.

The wrong gas settings can often cause this issue, as can dirty glassware, and it can be quite an unnerving sight to be greeted with after expecting to be served a beautiful, velvety-smooth pint of plain. It's an absolute nightmare for people with trypophobia (a fear of bubbles and holes), which must be an unnerving phobia to deal with when drinking somewhere new – how can they know they're not going to throw some bubbles your way?

Despite my strong feelings on the subject, I very, very rarely send back pints. I know plenty of people who will send back pints that are poured badly, I think there's a fine line between being arsey about it, and having a legitimate reason to ask for a repair. My criteria is usually that if I think it's bad enough to be posted on Shit London Guinness, it's probably bad enough to be returned for a replacement pint. Saying that, it had been years since I had returned a poor pint up until recently. I'm a non-confrontational man to my core, happy to eat the wrong meal or drink the wrong drink rather than say anything most of the time. I reckon if I was allergic to nuts, I'd quietly go more and more purple out of politeness rather than make any call for help.

Saying that, on my way home to Cork to take the first stab at writing this book, I ended up running into one of my best friends in Stansted Airport. I'm not sure if it was the couple of pints we'd had, the only benefit of a late evening's delayed flight, or the fact that I was stressing about having to go write a book all about how some pints are good, some are bad, here's where to drink them and here's their history, but after being served a pint that had a head full of bubbles – a pint so

Large heads on pints, however, aren't something that you want – you don't want to be half-drowning by the time you battle through the head, your nostrils engulfed in a foamy sea, and manage to drink any liquid.

offensive that even I wouldn't be able to drink it – I decided now was the time to stand up for myself. I'd paid my good, hard-earned money for this inflated-priced airport pint and I wanted to get a quality product in return. I ended up asking the bartender if they'd pour me another, mentioning there could be something wrong with the keg. They did but I was handed another Aero-looking monstrosity across the bar. I just gave up, resigned to never trying to return a pint again.

THE WRONG GLASS

I've often received criticism for being pedantic after posting pictures of 'bad' pints that are bad mainly because they've been served in something like a Fosters or Rekorderlig glass. When you order a pint of Guinness, you, and Guinness itself, expect to be served a decent pint of Guinness in a branded stout glass.

I swear I'm not being pedantic – and I have no issue with getting a 'milk' stout glass, one that is unbranded but still tulip shaped – but there is a science behind it. The tulip-shaped glasses have a wider top and a narrower base, a design which promotes the nucleation of the nitrogen bubbles and helps give Guinness its distinctive head. As it's poured, the wider top creates a sort of drag, which helps create the cascading effect you see on a pint of Guinness as it begins to settle. That doesn't happen if you just pour it into a regular lager glass, and is why you so often end up with a large head on a pint served in those glasses.

DIRTY GLASSES

Guinness needs to be poured into an extremely clean glass. It's one of the most important factors – it doesn't matter how clean your beer lines are, how perfect your gas settings are, or if the bartender has spent seventeen years working in the most prestigious Dublin pub and has poured over 100,000 perfect pints in their lifetime: if you're pouring a pint into a dirty glass, you're going to have a bad time.

Pouring pints into dirty glasses can cause unpleasant bubbles to form on the head, too large a head or too small, as well as numerous other issues. Have you ever been served a pint and seen little marks of dirt on the side of the glass, blemishes that make the ruby-red liquid look off? That's from an unclean glass. I'll always remember being invited to a pub north of the river that rates itself as having the best Guinness in London and being served a pint of Guinness in the dirtiest glass I've ever encountered. Grease

I know plenty of people
who will send back pints
that are poured badly
– I think there's a fine
line between being arsey
about it, and having a
legitimate reason to ask
for a repair.

and residue wrapped around the pint like a blanket of sadness. I reckon it must have been filled with gravy and given a quick rinse before being handed to me.

The big problem, I reckon, with that pub's Guinness, and something that is a big factor in glass cleanliness in general, is that the Guinness glasses are being washed in the same washer as the plates and cutlery used for food. The food oil, residue and debris end up clinging to the glass, and while it looks clean once it's taken out, the dirt reveals itself once the Guinness hits the glass – a discovery as disheartening as those people who buy concert tickets to see The Red Hot Chilli Pipers expecting to get the American funk-rock band, and end up seeing three Scottish lads playing the bagpipes.

Some pubs will have a separate washer entirely, one only used for Guinness glasses, and good for them. If you're looking to clean your glasses at home, the key is to wash them with scalding water, hand dry with a tea towel, give it a rinse and let it drip dry. Lovely.

WHAT MAKES A GOOD PINT

☐ Domed Head

☐ The Right Glass

☐ Lacing/Stick

☐ Taste

DOMED HEAD

Beautiful presentation is what sets Guinness apart from other beers and gives it its distinctive appeal. You want the pint to have 12–18mm of head, with the sweet spot being around 15mm, and to have the head sticking slightly out up over the rim of the glass to give it that domed head we all associate with a pint well poured. The Guinness quality team, with whom I once had a very educational day out at a few pubs, even have a special head-measuring tool. As I type these words, I can kind of see why some lager drinkers despise Guinness drinkers with a passion.

THE RIGHT GLASS

As I mentioned, you need the correct glassware to ensure the best pint. A tulip glass or nothing.

LACING/STICK

Lacing is the delicate pattern of foam left over on the inside of a glass once a pint has been drunk. The tell-tale sign of a pint poured well – and enjoyed – is if there is lacing present on the side of the glass when you've finished. A well-looked-after line poured into a clean glass should leave behind a pattern of residual foam on the inside of the glass.

The lacing on a pint of Guinness tells a story in much the same way as the rings of a tree do. We can tell a tree's age from the rings in its stump, and we can learn much about how a pint has been drunk from lacing. The markings on the side of a finished Guinness glass can show us how quickly a pint was drunk: if there are four markings, we can tell that it was drunk by a thirsty man in five gulps, with ten marks, it was finished in eleven sips, and so on. A Guinness with general lacing, but no distinct marks that show where sups ended, tells us that the person who devoured it could only quench their thirst by drinking it all in one go.

We can tell a tree's age from the rings in its stump, and we can learn much about how a pint has been drunk from lacing.

TASTE

A good pint of Guinness should taste like Guinness. It's a simple thing to say, but as discussed there are some factors that can interfere with the end product if a pub is lazy or doesn't care about the quality of their pint. Good pints of plain don't need bells or whistles, light shows or fireworks, they should just taste as they're meant to – smooth, creamy, very slightly bitter, with a subtle sweetness. By God, I'm making myself thirsty.

The Guinness pour is an important part of what makes it so special. No other alcohol brand has such a ritual surrounding it – no one really cares how a lager is poured as long as it's not flat and doesn't have a ridiculous-sized head. The ceremony of the pour is probably a part of what endears the drink to so many people: whether you're conscious of it or not, it does make you feel like there's some sort of extra quality control going on here that you are not privy to. Surely if my pint takes five times as long to pour as the fella standing at the bar next to me it should taste better, right?

I've been thinking of a few acts that remind me of the pouring of a Guinness. Acts in life that have majesty and a sense that you're waiting for something, that you're invested in the final result. Things like these:

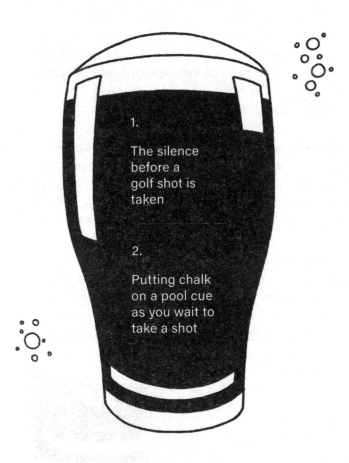

1.

The silence before a golf shot is taken

2.

Putting chalk on a pool cue as you wait to take a shot

3.

Standing up on a train by the door as it approaches your stop

4.

The last five minutes of waiting before a game is installed and you can click play

5.

Waiting for someone to call your all-in while you have a perfect poker hand

I've always given a bit of a shrugged-shoulders response when I'm asked why the two-part pouring of a Guinness matters so much. Usually it's by one of my slightly annoyed beer-drinking friends who isn't used to that 119.5-second wait (that's the official, recommended time: just a fraction under two minutes) from when the first part of the pint is poured to when the finished product is ready. I think it's an attention span issue. Like much of the world these days, lager drinkers are too used to instant gratification. They want their pints and they want them now. They're used to having their greedy lips around the rim of a cold glass within 45 seconds of ordering that pint, not understanding the contemplative joy in those 119.5 seconds of solace at the bar.

Sometimes, when it hasn't been your round for a while, it's nice to have that time at the bar to reset and ground yourself a little. It's important to check in on yourself. How are you feeling? All good? Do we want to slow it down, or speed it up? Feeling sleepy or feeling like you want to sing Westlife in a Soho karaoke bar? Are we bound for a disco-ball illuminated club or will the only fluorescent lights we encounter tonight be the semi-dilapidated, dimly lit kebab-shop sign? I can cover just about all of that in those 119.5 seconds. Just as my mouth begins to water at the thought of an encounter with a drunken doner, the pint is ready to be lofted diligently back to the table. Mighty stuff.

That may sound simple, or perhaps slightly unnerving, but once you've poured a couple it feels like riding a bike and you can pour them fairly handily. That is, unless you're like me, and end up messing up a pour live on *This Morning*, one of the UK's most watched television programmes. Though I've never worked in a pub, I'd poured a fair few pints at this stage, mainly through partnership work I've done with Guinness – I poured a couple on a day out with the quality team, made a couple of videos of pours using their new Nitrosurge, poured a few in pubs despite my protests, and let's not forget my previously mentioned foray into the harsh world of TV advertising.

But on St Patrick's Day 2023, despite a rushed backstage refresher with the Guinness team, I managed to overpour a pint on live television while Dermot O'Leary and Alison Hammond looked on in horror. I was going for the domed head but the lights, the camera and the pressure got to me on the big stage. I ended up having to post the picture of my own pint disaster on Shit London Guinness. An honourable man must fall on his own sword and embrace his mistakes.

THE POUR

Anyway – the two-part pour. Why do they do it? What's the point? Well, before we look at the why, let's look at the how. How do you pour a pint of Guinness?

You often hear people say now that the two-part pour is a marketing gimmick and doesn't make any difference to the end result of a pint. The two-part pour *is* a legacy method, dating back as far as the 1930s when Guinness had two types of casks: highly conditioned and low-conditioned. They were kept at different pressures, the high-pressured, lively barrel being used to fill the glass with a foamy head, while the low barrel was used to add the stout to the bottom. The excess head was then scraped off the top. I'd highly recommend looking up a couple of YouTube videos to see how it was done – it was no easy task for sure, and much more complicated than the modern pour.

When the great Michael Ash and the Guinness brewery team solved the two-keg problem by having the brainwave to use nitrogen to produce draught Guinness, the pour using two barrels stopped. So why are we still pouring in two parts these days? Shouldn't it be abandoned as a relic of the past? No, and I'll explain why. It's all in the head.

As previously mentioned, when pouring a pint of Guinness, we want to achieve that domed head of 12–18mm. During the first pour, the beer is gently introduced to the glass at an angle, activating the nitrogen bubbles and helping them rise to the

**Surely if my pint takes
five times as long
to pour as the fella
standing at the bar next
to me it should taste
better, right?**

surface to create that creamy head. Allowing that to settle before the second pour helps the head to form first, so that it ends up smooth, creamy and velvety. If pints were poured in one go, they'd all have huge heads and you would have to manoeuvre your way through a sea of foam every time you wanted to take a sup of your pint. Nobody wants that. Guinness's marketing has really leaned into the two-part pour, with iconic slogans like 'Good things come to those who wait', which help reinforce the pint as a product so perfect that it's worth waiting for.

Obviously, you don't *need* two-part-pour pints of Guinness to enjoy it. If you have a keg and want to pour all the Jimmy Neutron pints your heart desires – go for it. You also don't need to season your food. You don't need to put butter on your toast. But you should.

5.

Beautiful Pints & Where to Find Them

It's hard to describe a pub as 'good' or 'bad'. Like all things, pubs are subjective and depend on what each person cares about and values. Do they want peace and quiet? Do they want to have a boogie? Do they want to stand on a table and sing 'Angels' by Robbie Williams without the fear of reproach? It all depends. One person's favourite pub might be my personal idea of hell and vice versa. Different strokes for different folks, as they say.

I can only speak for myself and what I like in a pub. I often get asked to put together my 'Top 10 Pubs in London for a Guinness' and get accosted in the comments for not including someone's favourite pub in the list, some place where they claim the pints taste like they've come directly from the teat of the cow born closest to St James's Gate. A lot of the time I've just never been to the pub they've mentioned. I'd have heard about them before, the whisper of a decent pint living deep in the annals of my iPhone Notes app where the name was drunkenly typed outside Brixton station at 3 a.m. as the scent of roasted, sweet & salty peanuts and pungent skunk filled the air.

Lost knowledge that will never be revisited, unless I somehow end up two hours across London from where I live and wander into an old Irish pub whose name rings a bell, an ancient wisdom only drawn upon in the most vital moments.

That said, if you're not near one of my actual recommendations, I've attempted to break down the most important elements which, to me, constitute a good pub, as well as the obvious markers of pubs to be avoided.

THINGS I LOVE IN PUBS

• THE CLIENTELE

The people make a pub. What is a pub without its orchestra – the sounds of laughter, anger, rage, love, heartbreak, sorrow, joy? It is empty both physically and philosophically without the right punters.

A pub, for me, needs to be filled with people who are all generally on the same page. But the page

of my favourite pub doesn't need to bear the same words and notations as my second favourite pub, and that is what makes the tapestry of them so beautiful. Whether the hymn we're all singing is 'let's quietly drink and watch the match' or 'we will all sit here and drink five to six pints with our friends until the seventh drink where we will all gather together to sing Westlife', it's important to me that it's not interrupted by any outliers. I don't want to be washing my hands in the bathroom at half-time in one of my favourite pubs and have some wide-eyed fella called Hugo telling me about his properties in Clapham and wanting to have a fight with me. There's pubs for that and this isn't one of them – we're all on the same page here, brother.

Whether the people in a pub are seven auld fellas, sat on the same high stool they've been strength-ening their groove into for the last decade while watching their team lose again and again, or a leafy pub garden full of creative twenty/thirty-somethings talking about their latest Hinge escapade, I have time for most clientele, but with the right pub for each one. No invaders, please.

▪ **THE PINT**

We've talked about this at length already, but it would be remiss of me to build a reputation for criticising/praising pints and not briefly touch on it when talking about my criteria for a great pub. I am writing a book about them, after all. It's quite simple – a good pub will serve good beer. They'll care about their lines, how their beer is kept, the general cleanliness of the set-up and how their customers receive their pint. Good pubs serve good pints.

▪ THE SEATS

I like a high stool at the bar. I don't particularly like to sit at them: such honours are reserved for the pint-men of legend, those who would live a glorious life in Valhalla after a life well spent if we were Vikings and drinking pints of plain was combat, but I like them to be there. They reassure

me about a pub – there is space here for people who like to sit up at the bar, drink, have a chat, and we won't be rid of the stools so more of you people can tap your hands on the bar in impatience. Wait your turn.

THINGS I LIKE IN PUBS

And now, on to the good-to-haves, things that are not necessarily deal-breakers but which I would make sure I'd have in my perfect pub. Doing all of these right can be what turns a good pub into a great pub.

▪ THE TELLY

A telly can be the centrepiece that brings the clientele of a pub together. Much like punters would gather around a fire for warmth in public houses and taverns of old, some sport shown on a gargantuan widescreen can warm the cockles of many. One of the great joys of life is gathering around a circular pub table with the lads, and many others, all cricking your necks towards a spectacle in unison. It can be the spark that sets a night alight, a big win that sends you into silly-land, where shots of sambuca and a late-night

I would love nothing more, completely earnestly and unironically, than to meet some friends on a weekday evening to drink three to five pints and watch an entire five-episode saga of *Four In A Bed* or *Come Dine With Me.*

karaoke bar in Soho await, or the dampener that makes the rest of your pints taste bitter and dampens the joy in your soul.

A great London pub, Molly Bloom's in Dalston (see p. 120), has so many screens showing so many various sports that I once, while sat at a table alone nursing a pint of plain, was able to watch

horse racing, hurling and the Premier League all at once without even needing to move my head. That is what peak performance looks like.

The telly is under-utilised in the modern pub. I obviously love watching big matches on it and things like that, but I've seen a few clips online of people gathered in the local on a Tuesday night watching *Harry Potter* or *The Chase* together. That sounds lovely to me. I would love nothing more, completely earnestly and unironically, than to meet some friends on a weekday evening to drink three to five pints and watch an entire five-episode saga of *Four In A Bed* or *Come Dine With Me*. Forget pub quizzes – bring the customers in to guess the ratings of B&Bs in Chester. You would be printing money.

▪ THE SMOKING AREA

One of my major vices, other than the fact that I am fond of a drop and I enjoy watching professional wrestling, is that I like to smoke a few cigarettes on a night out. I was a 'sober smoker', a phrase used by those who tell people they've fully quit but still have to tick '1–2 a week' in the smoking section on health forms. I smoked around seventeen to twenty-four, but gave up once the first COVID lockdown hit and I was too lazy to keep walking downstairs from my third-floor flat. I truly believe that before then I only smoked during the day so I had an excuse to take lots of breaks from work. Those five minutes of doom-scrolling as the people walking past silently judged me were important to me at the time.

A smoking area doesn't need to be all glitz and glamour. It doesn't need to have 700 seats and a fella named Giuseppe out in the back making authentic Neapolitan pizzas out of a refurbished shipping container. I just like it to be there, so that it can facilitate one of the greatest combinations of the modern world: drinking pints, smoking cigarettes and talking shite.

Although I don't think it necessarily needs to be a sprawling, multi-tiered, flowery jungle like that of the Faltering Fullback in Finsbury Park (see p. 114), it certainly does help. Smoking gardens fill extremely quickly in the summer, especially around London, as punters seek to engage in the sacred trio of fun.

• THE STAFF

Having friendly, kind and helpful staff can make or break a pub. It's important to feel like a pub actually cares about my custom. I completely appreciate that some people behind the bar might not care too much about making people feel like that if they're not fussed about the job, but the staff in pubs that do really make it shine are the ones who make me want to keep coming back.

A bad interaction, conversely, can completely turn me off a pub. I'm a big fan of holding a grudge, many of my friends call me Grudge Ryan, but why would I ever go back to a pub if I feel like I'm going to be on edge or annoyed? A great example is a pub – which will not be named – that I used to frequent near where I live. I drank there for years, but one evening a bartender was being completely creepy and leery towards all of the women in our group, so we left and I've just never gone back. Why would I when that's the kind of people they have working in there?

▪ **POOL TABLE**

There's nothing better than an evening of playing pool with the lads. Simple.

THINGS I HATE IN PUBS

On the other hand, there are certain things that can wreck a good pub experience. Things like:

▪ FRUIT MACHINES

Let's be real, they are a bit sad. Let's leave them where they belong – back in 2010, when *Lost* last aired on TV.

▪ OVERPRICED FOOD

Pubs need to stop pretending that their chips are so artisanal that they warrant a £7 price point. I don't care how much organic sea salt you've used. I know you got them from Iceland.

▪ KIDS

I know what you're thinking. What a grumpy man. He can't even bring himself to pretend that it's not annoying when darling River is running around a pub and misbehaving for Mummy. Well, tough. I'm not saying they should be banned from pubs, but all I'm saying is that I've never seen a child in any of my favourite pubs. There's a correlation there.

• SELLING/RENTING CHARGING PACKS

If you see a pub selling or renting charging packs, run. It's probably a tourist trap. A good pub will just plug your phone in behind the bar in times of need.

• LOUD MUSIC

There is no need to be blasting George Ezra while I'm trying to discuss whether Roy Keane would make a good politician or not with my friends.

• ONLY USING STRAIGHT GLASSES

Pure laziness, in my opinion. Get the right glasses for the right drinks or don't bother. At that point, just use plastic and tell me to do one while you hand it to me.

• OUTDOOR BENCHES INSIDE

Please just shell out for a proper table. Outdoor benches should live outdoors.

But enough of all that, where are these perfect pubs? In reality, I find it hard to call any one pub my 'favourite' or say that 'X' pub has the best pint of Guinness. Taste is subjective and my favourite pub changes from year to year. There will most certainly be people reading this and cursing me for leaving their favourite pub off the list, but unfortunately I probably just haven't been there, or maybe caught them on an off-day for a pint of Guinness.

This list is also inevitably biased towards the places I've lived (i.e. London, Cork) and the places I've been, but I've tried to include something for everyone. There's also a bunch I've had to leave off before this book became the size of a Brandon Sanderson novel.

Sorry.

LONDON

London is where I presently lay my head, and while there are always things to complain about and Londoners to make those complaints, it does have some excellent pubs.

The Sheephaven Bay

2 Mornington Street, Camden Town, London, NW1 7QD, England

The Sheephaven has slowly but surely become my favourite pub over the last few years. The staff there are outstanding – genuine, caring, kind people who look after their regulars alongside serving the throngs of punters who arrive from all over the country to sample their fabled pint of Guinness – the five-minute walk from Camden or Mornington Crescent tube stations becoming a Camino de Pintofplaino for many.

The pint in there is top tier – one of the best in London. They pride themselves on their Guinness and that's why it is so heavily touted as one of the city's top locations for it. All pints are served in old-style tulip glasses and they even have a choice between a regular or extra cold tap, which is the mark of a pub that really puts effort into its Guinness.

It also combines two other important pub factors, tellies and smoking areas, in one by having an incredible smoking area out the back with two large tellies in it. I've seen

some great crowds out there watching the Cheltenham horse races, rugby, football… it always draws a crowd for sports. The Sheephaven Bay is also inexplicably the supporters' pub for Atlético de Madrid in London. I never realised this until a friend asked me to recommend a quiet pub on a Tuesday night to read his book and drink some Guinness and I received a text asking why there was a throng of red-and-white jerseys crowded into the backroom screaming. I suppose the jerseys hung up on the wall should have been a giveaway, but the Sheephaven is already one of the most maximalist pubs I've ever visited – almost every inch of the walls is covered with some variety of football/rugby/GAA jersey/scarf/poster, so it's easy to miss a jersey amongst the rest.

One of my favourite memories of this pub is being one of the last people standing (or sitting, in this case) after a long, long St Patrick's Day, as the last pints of the night were served, those final nightcaps before we waddled off to our slumber, and ending up trying to sing traditional Irish songs with the table next to us. We were all quite drunk, quite bad at singing and only able to remember about 25 per cent of the lyrics, but it was a beautiful time as we slapped our hands on our knees and mumbled through the tale of the wild rover who spent all his money on whiskey and beer.

The Twelve Pins

263 Seven Sisters Rd, Finsbury Park, London, N4 2DE, England

'The Pins' is a pub just by Finsbury Park station, and both suffers and benefits from the association of being a pub that's 'just by the station'. Whenever I mention the Pins, people ask me if that's 'the pub by the station' and say they've never wandered in because it's so chaotic around there. But it has its benefits – because it's so close, people can pop in for a drink before their train quite easily. Swings and roundabouts.

Anyway, the Pins is a classic Irish pub and a true Arsenal boozer. It will show GAA as long as there isn't an Arsenal match on, in which case

the place will be overrun by a sea of red and not somewhere you want to be unless you're a Gunner. I always recommend it as a nice place to have a really solid pint of Guinness, but by God be sure to check there isn't a match on before you go.

They have always been very good to me in there, making sure I was able to get a table for a group back when you weren't allowed to freely walk around the bar with COVID regulations. I also had my first experience with being charged a 'regular's price' in the Pins. I noticed that my friends were being charged around 50p more than myself for each pint in their rounds, and one day when I asked why, they let me know it was because I was a regular. It's always nice to be rewarded for being fond of a drop in there on my way home from work.

The Auld Shillelagh

105 Stoke Newington Church St, London, N16 0UD, England

The Auld Shil is always a great shout for the highly contested prize of the best pint in London. The pint in there is so good that sometimes I wish other people didn't actually know about it, so that I would be able to get a seat a bit easier. I'd almost be tempted to slander it on my accounts so that people might stop going there and I could stroll in on a Saturday night, sit in some prime real-estate smoking-area seating and sup away in peace, but that's a heel turn I'm not willing to make yet.

It's quite a small, narrow pub, but the layout makes up for that – they have separators and cubbies throughout so while you do generally sit quite close to the other punters, there is a

feeling of relative privacy when sat in the cubs. The smoking area in the Shil has changed quite a bit over the years – what was once a small yard with a couple of unloved-looking tables out the back has been transformed into a really solid area with a multitude of tables, all alongside heaters and a retractable roof for the inevitable rain.

One of my biggest regrets in life is missing the night that John Cena and Jason Momoa dropped in for a few pints of Guinness. I was absolutely gutted when I saw pictures of them sitting in one of the spots I have occupied so many times during my years in London. I'm not even bothered about Jason to be honest, but John Cena was my childhood hero and is an all-round great man with everything he does for Make-A-Wish, and I'd have loved to have bought him a pint. Fingers crossed that day might come, and he can give me an AA through a table full of pints of Guinness out the back of the Shil. That's a bump I'd happily take.

The Cock Tavern

23 Phoenix Rd, London, NW1 1HB, England

The Cock is a perfect example of never judging a book by its cover. Well, you can kind of judge it by its cover, in that from the outside it looks like a rough-and-ready boozer that you might be wary of entering, but is actually a friendly, no-frills, working-class, left-leaning Irish boozer where you will always be welcomed. It's a flat-top pub near Euston

SLIGEACH
SLIGO 2

station that, I believe, has fought to keep its building from being bought up by property developers as the rest of the Euston/King's Cross area has been stripped of its character – lost to high-rise office buildings and flats. The Cock sits proud as a bastion of old working-class London – somewhere that can't be brushed aside to make way for investment properties majority owned by foreign development funds.

The owner, Sheila, is a down-to-earth Sligo woman and loves to chat to people who approach the bar. It's the same for everyone else who works there and it's obvious that most of the staff are either some sort of family or friends of Sheila's. The pint is exceptional, and cheap for London standards. It is also the meeting place of the RMT union and home to the London Celtic supporters club, who come out in throngs anytime they play.

The Crown

418 Mare St, London, E8 1HP, England

I'll always remember the Crown as the pub where one of my friends, a Donegal man by birth, told the bar lady where he was from and she responded by stating 'The biggest dick I've ever encountered in my life was a Donegal man's.' Bewildered, he took the pints back down the table and told us the story, which made us howl with laughter and endeared the pub to us for ever more. The beautiful pints of Guinness they serve certainly help.

A true local's pub, the Crown is where I've had the most chats up at the bar while waiting for a pint in my entire life. In most London pubs there could be eight lads all waiting for a pint to be served to them at once, and absolutely zero chance that anyone would have a chat with them. That all goes out the window here. The old boys ask where you're from, your plans for the night, what you think of the pub; it's great and always leads to some interesting, yet chaotic, conversations. It is also the only pub I know that has Astroturf in the smoking area.

They also do tapas, but just completely unprompted and free. That's the beauty of a true Irish pub, not an 'Irish pub' like O'Neills but an *Irish* Irish pub. You generally get dropped down some food, probably with the intention of lining your stomach so you're able to survive long enough to buy more drink, but you wouldn't be getting that in the plastic places. They'd charge ya £7 for a bowl of chips and spit on it on the way down.

The Crown is the only place in my entire

twenty-eight years on this earth where I've been served slices of ham on skewers. Sitting there, supping away, we were handed a plate of 'funeral sandwiches' as they are known in Ireland, small triangle-shaped sandwiches, cocktail sausages and some ham skewers – just a few slices of ham on cocktail sticks. Incredible stuff. It also displays its *Four In A Bed* winner's plaque proudly on the bar – an episode I ashamedly must admit I have not watched, but one I need to as soon as this book is written. It must be incredible. Were the guests, likely posh Sussex B&B hosts, impressed enough by the ham skewers to give them top marks? I hope so.

Coach & Horses

42 Wellington St, London, WC2E 7BD, England

So far, none of the pubs I've listed are in central London. As a London resident that's quite normal – I very rarely go into central London just to have a pint, but at the same time, if you're working or meeting friends around there after work, it's very important to have a solid pub in your arsenal that you can call upon when needed. For me, that's the Coach & Horses, a very small pub just off Covent Garden. It serves lovely pints of plain. It has a quaint interior – felt stools, red carpet, inscribed mirrors – and is quite small, so you either need to be lucky or get there relatively early to grab a seat. I've always loved it as a spot to sneak away for an early finish

pint with colleagues and I know, even now that I've left, that my ex-colleagues still carry on that tradition. In true central London style, you can always stand outside if you can't grab a seat, which allows for some great people-watching as the crowds dash through Covent Garden, each person looking more stressed than the last while you quietly sup in peace.

Note the address, though – there are several pubs with the same name in central London and in my opinion, only two of them are ever worth visiting: this one and 'the red one', sometimes called Norman's, in Soho. Wellington Street has the good Guinness and the red one has the craic and history. Look up Norman's – it's got a fascinating story and is a great pub to this day – but Wellington Street is the best. The rest of the C&Hs around central London are best avoided.

The Guinea Grill

30 Bruton Pl, London, W1J 6NL, England

I've never felt more looked after in my life than at the Guinea Grill. It is a Mayfair institution, claiming to have been a pub since 1423, and serves one of the best pints of Guinness in London. It combines being both a high-class restaurant and a Guinness-first pub perfectly – with the bar at the front and the restaurant in the back, and facing onto a very quiet side street so you can drink outside in relative peace without having to worry about being smashed into by a car every seventeen seconds. The food is of the same standard as the pints of plain: an incredible menu with the most knowledgeable staff I've ever encountered. The prices mirror the quality but it's an amazing place to eat on a special occasion, and to drink on any.

All of my experiences in the Guinea were while Oisin Rogers was in charge, a legendary pub manager and absolute gentleman, who has recently departed to run his own establishment (the Devonshire in Soho, as yet unopened, but which I'm sure will be incredible) but has left behind a wonderful team. I am very fond of

Oisin, a larger-than-life man who owns any room he steps into and has always made me feel so welcome and looked after in the Guinea. I think the era of true hospitality masters is diminishing as the years go by, but Oisin continues to lead the gold standard, one hand on the Guinness tap and the other conducting while he tells tales across the bar.

Gibney's

70 City Rd, London, EC1Y 2BJ, England

I'm not just being an arsehole when I call Gibney's an underground pub for a great pint of Guinness – it is literally under the ground. The sister pub of Gibney's in Dublin, the London version sits under Daffodil Mulligans, a restaurant from Michelin-starred chef Richard Mulligan, which serves high-quality Irish-inspired cuisine. As the bar food in Gibney's comes directly from the restaurant, it's safe to say it's the best in the entire city. One of the most beautiful parts of the pub are the snugs with tellies: I've watched a bunch of matches in these, sat with seven or eight mates all supping incredible pints of stout and watching football on the big screens. You can even close the door to the snug if you are so inclined, privacy-wise, but I lean more on the side of gloating that you've managed to snag it when disappointed faces peer in to see if it's free.

Gibney's shines bright in a sea of generic,

overpriced, boring bars and pubs in Shoreditch (can you tell I'm not a fan of the area?). Cormac Gibney, the pub landlord, is one of the nicest people I've ever had the pleasure of meeting and takes care of both his punters and his Guinness, ensuring everyone is looked after and the pints are flowing nicely. It's also the first pub on this list that does a late trade – you could be supping pints in Gibney's until the clock strikes 2 a.m. and you are well and truly oiled.

The Faltering Fullback

19 Perth Rd, Finsbury Park, London, N4 3HB, England

The Fullback has the best pub garden in London, bar none. It's a sprawling, multi-tiered, green wonderland that I'd describe as being like if Rivendell and the Shire had a child but it was a beer garden out the back of a pub in north London. It also serves a very decent pint of plain and shows all of the sports, including GAA. Food-wise, there is a very nice Thai kitchen in the Fullback – a combination that is present in quite a few Irish pubs around London and one I'm not sure I have an explanation for yet. Either way, it is class. Out front, there is actually a clipping of an article where I mentioned them having one of the best pints in the city. I was very pleasantly surprised while absent-mindedly reading the various posters and cut-outs on the wall to find my name.

I'd go here as often as I could, especially in the summer, if it wasn't so busy. Legendary for its incredible beer garden, I would recommend

getting here quite early to make sure you get a spot, because those seats fill up quickly. I've also hidden a cut-out of John Cena from a WWE Top Trumps card game in one of the DVDs they have at the top of the smoking area – if you manage to find this please let me know and I will send you a T-shirt or something. I think it was in *Lord of the Rings:* *The Fellowship of the Ring*, or else *Band of Brothers* Season One, but I can't be sure. Have fun looking.

Skehans

1 Kitto Rd, London, SE14 5SN, England

Mentioning Skehans is a solid segue from speaking about the Fullback

because it's actually run by the same Limerick-born brothers. As of writing, it has just won the award for best pub in London. Considering there are over 3,500 of them in the city, that is no mean feat, and it is well deserved: Skehans has a solid pint of Guinness and an even better pub garden. Having a pool table is a massive plus in my books, too.

Shepherd and Flock

84 Goldhawk Rd, London, W12 8HA, England

The Shepherd and Flock is a solid, no-nonsense boozer in west London. I used to work near Westfield in White City and it was always my spot for a pint after work. It sells good Guinness for a cheap price – expect no more and no less.

Stop in by Mr Falafel in Shepherd's Bush market to line the stomach before you head for a pint and get the best falafel wrap in all of London. What a day out.

The Hercules (FKA Tommy Flynn's)

504 Holloway Rd, London, N7 6JA, England

Holloway Road is an absolutely elite spot for pints of Guinness. There is an incredible number of pubs, sixteen in total – a number I recently learned while doing a two-day pub crawl up it over the bank holiday weekends. I had been shooting a video to show off all of what Holloway Road has to offer, but as we ended up only managing twelve on the first day, followed by a very slow and pained four on the following, I'm not sure that footage is fit to see the light of day.

Anyway, the Hercules is a great, family-run Irish pub. It is a perfect spot to get away from it all and watch the match while sinking a few beautiful pints of Guinness. They're great for late night entertainment, always getting in Irish musicians and the like. Proper boozer stuff. One of my best nights there was watching a vampire Elvis impersonator do a set on Halloween – the drink was flowing and the following morning I was all shook up (a-huh-huh).

The Crown

622 Holloway Rd, Archway, London, N19 3PA, England

Unlike the Crown Guesthouse in Hackney, mentioned above, I don't believe anyone has ever slept at this Crown intentionally, though it is certainly the kind of place you could fall soundly to sleep in after a prolonged day supping pints of plain and playing darts. A true boozer to its core, the Crown isn't somewhere you come to drink natural wine and neck artisan olives stuffed with the finest blue cheese, sold by someone for £15,000 a pound in a Hackney public-school, trust-fund cheese shop. You come here to drink pints, watch sport, play darts or pool and if you don't like it, you know where the door is.

The Crown is possibly the most uninviting pub on this list and that's what makes it special. With perpetually closed doors and frosted

windows, it's impossible to know whether the pub is full, quiet, on fire, closed or otherwise until you push through those doors. I love a pub where every patron turns to query your arrival as soon as they hear the doors open – who is this person? Have I seen them before? It's a pub for locals and they appreciate it because of that. One of my favourite parts of bringing people to the Crown is showing them the smoking area. It's basically a prison yard: a tiny pavemented area just next to the toilets, surrounded by grey, concrete walls stained by time. There is also a net of sorts, 10ft up, to catch what I can only assume to be the general debris that falls upon a place as blighted as Holloway Road. God himself casts rubbish from the skies upon its accursed boozers.

Saying that, once you get inside, the bar staff are very kind and the pints are both incredible and cheap. It's one of the best pints I've had outside of Ireland. They exclusively use the old-style glasses, which I always appreciate.

Molly Bloom's

525 Kingsland Rd, London, E8 4AR, England

Molly Bloom's is a proper working-class Irish pub situated at the heart of the wave of gentrification in Dalston. Painted an incredibly bright shade of green, it's hard to miss among the dreary grey buildings that surround it. It pours a solid, cheap pint and I reckon it has the largest number of screens per square metre (SPSM?) of all the London pubs. I fail to see how Apple's new VR headset can succeed when you can get that same experience for the price of a pint and the overground over to Molly Bloom's.

THE REST OF THE UK

I have, unfortunately, not had the opportunity to travel the length and breadth of the country on the hunt for the most glorious pint, though I've been lucky enough to encounter some beauties.

The Royal Oak

1 Infirmary St, Edinburgh, EH1 1LT, Scotland

Edinburgh blew me away when I visited there for the first time in 2021, and this pub was a big part of it. I was doing a pub crawl and posting about the pints of Guinness on social media and I came across the Royal Oak, a very small, square, one-room pub with space for maybe twenty-five people and a bar facing the seats. Ordinarily a pub that plays traditional folk music, the sessions had stopped due to

COVID by the time I had arrived, but from talking to the people in there, I can say they sound great and are surely running again by now.

It's the perfect place to strike up a conversation – I was solo in Edinburgh, stopping by before seeing friends in Glasgow, and the smallness of the pub basically forces you into a conversation with your fellow patrons. I met some great characters in there,

people that I chatted to each time I went back (three times in two days!) and I'd suggest anyone visiting Edinburgh stop in for a natter.

It's by far the best pint in the city and is somewhere I'd love to visit again soon. I'd also recommended stopping by the Indian restaurant next door for an incredible curry before, during, or after a visit to the Royal Oak.

Kay's Bar

39 Jamaica St, Edinburgh, EH3 6HF, Scotland

I really loved Kay's Bar, a place that was recommended to me many times when I asked my followers where I should stick my head in while I was visiting Edinburgh. Sitting slightly outside of the city centre, Kay's is a great little pub with massive character of its own, as well as being filled with them. They take great care with their pints of Guinness and it's up there for one of the best pints in the city. My lasting memory is of spending forty-five minutes discussing the managerial career and tactical prowess of ex-Ireland manager Martin O'Neill. I'd recommend Martin as a discussion topic for any drunken reveller visiting Kay's.

The Laurieston Bar

58 Bridge St, Glasgow, G5 9HU, Scotland

One thing I didn't realise until I walked in the door of the Laurieston, the pub that came most highly recommended to me in Glasgow, was that it was the location for the scene in *Succession* where Roman sees football club Hearts on the telly, leading him to mistake them for the team his father supports (actually their bitter rivals, Hibs) and buying them as a bizarre present. I'm a huge fan of the show and that gave the pub top marks before I'd even tasted the pint of plain.

This is a legendary Glasgow pub, a real, friendly, genuine place with a great atmosphere that needs to be visited to be experienced. Pretty much unchanged since the 1960s, it has a large island bar, red carpets and curtains and retro-style furnishing, with old photos and signs hung up throughout. It is also a Category C listed building. It has a free jukebox, an ambitious 'indoor smoking room' and one of the best pints of Guinness I've had outside of Ireland. Lovely.

Heraghty's

708 Pollokshaws Rd, Glasgow, G41 2AD, Scotland

This is a gorgeous Irish pub which would not look out of place next to a Dublin pub like Kehoes or the Lord Edward. I am a sucker for a designed, frosted window and leather-backed seating in front of circular wooden tables, so Heraghty's is my cup of tea. It is an exceptionally friendly pub with a huge selection of whiskeys, as well as a top pint of Guinness.

The Fiddler's Elbow

11-12 Boyce's St, Brighton, BN1 1AN, England

There are many beautiful things to do, see and experience in Brighton and a pint of plain is not usually what springs to mind. Saying that, after a tiring day at the beach, playing games at the pier, bare-knuckle boxing a seagull for your last chip and dancing the night away at a club called Revenge (all of which I can speak about from personal experi-ence), there is nothing better than a pint of plain to nurse your injured soul.

The Fiddler's Elbow is the only Irish pub in Brighton, so it's not exactly fighting for competition to have the best pint of plain, but they really do have a beauty. It is a nice little place, bearing all of your standard Irish pub mainstays – Guinness posters, packets of Tayto (the wrong ones unfortunately, but that could be its own book) and trad, all of which I'm a big fan of. It's also the first

pub in years to refuse to serve me without ID, something that was annoying at the time but in hindsight quite nice, as I'm not sure that day will ever come again.

Mulligans

12 Southgate, Manchester, M3 2RB, England

Famously an old haunt of the Manchester United team and of fellow Cork man Roy Keane in particular, Mulligans is widely regarded as having the best pint of plain on offer in Manchester. They market themselves as 'The Home of Guinness in Manchester', a bold claim for sure, but one that I would heartily agree with. Mulligans pours one of the finest pints I've ever had in the UK. Fair warning, it's a busy aul spot. To get yourself a seat in one of their lovely booths, I would recommend the Gen Z method for getting front-of-stage spots for *The 1975* – be there early and be quick.

Lady Luck

18 St Peter's St, Canterbury, CT1 2BQ, England

I loved Canterbury when I spent a few days visiting there. A beautiful place with a rich history, I'd be seriously tempted to move out there if the train was about half an hour faster and there weren't 7 million students roaming the streets at any time (writing that sentence made me feel like an old man).

I ended up drinking in Lady Luck a couple of nights; it's a really cool rock bar that serves great food. As a metal fan, especially in my youth, I have a penchant for these kinds of pubs. They remind me of sneaking into the 18+ gigs like Enter Shikari in Cork and getting battered in mosh pits. To me, there is no

greater joy than drinking a pint while 'War Pigs' by Black Sabbath plays in the background. Much like Super Hans from Peep Show, I am usually completely opposed to being given a 'logo on the foam', a shamrock shape in the top of your pint, but Lady Luck changed the game for me by serving me a pentagram. I thought it was hilarious and created an exception to my rule – no logo in the foam, *unless* it's a pentagram. Rock and roll.

Shenanigans

77 Tithebarn St, Liverpool, L2 2EN, England

Liverpool is one of the greatest cities in the world. I've had friends living up there for years and we would end up finding ourselves darkening the doorstep of Shenanigans time and time again. It is an excellent pub – one full of characters, great staff and brave warriors on the hunt for the perfect pint of stout. The pub is relatively small, but has an upstairs bar and rooftop space to make up for it. It's the perfect spot for supping away on pints while watching the football and then spending the night enjoying some live music.

The Spotted Dog

104 Warwick St, Birmingham, B12 0NH, England

Birmingham is famously strongly connected to Ireland. The migration from the Famine brought many of us over, and by the 1960s one in six children born here had at least one Irish parent. As such, you'd think there'd be a few Irish pubs that are able to dish out a decent pint of Guinness, and you'd be correct.

The Spotted Dog brims with character. You don't see many pubs like this any more – a real pub for real people. Unassuming from the outside, inside it's quaint with a great selection of whiskeys and a creamy pint of Guinness that is absolutely the best in the city. The smoking area is also quite nice – a great spot, I found, for a discussion about the rise and fall of cash-for-gold shops during the recession.

The Star

539 Fishponds Rd, Bristol, BS16 3AF, England

One of the favoured pastimes of an Irish person abroad is to walk around different cities and make comparisons to places back home, mostly unfounded and untrue, but good fun all the same. There's a certain unexplainable joy in walking down a street in Zagreb, looking around and saying 'This is a bit like Glanmire' while you scratch your chin contemplatively. Try it some time.

With that in mind, here we go. Bristol is a bit like the British version of Galway. A bastion of hemp jumpers, white people with dreadlocks and posh students, it has the same reputation as being an incredible city to visit, but you will most definitely experience the pungent stench of skunk on each street corner and echoes of 'rah, where's my baccy?' ringing throughout the city. I have a great story about a misunderstanding late in the night at a house party between two of my friends, one Irish and one British, both misunderstanding what type of 'rah' people the other was talking about, but that is for another time.

Bristol is packed full of incredible pubs and bars, but the Star in Fishponds is definitely my favourite. It sits a ways outside of the city centre, but it is well worth the bus out if you are in search of a top pint of Guinness. Based on the method of old Irish working men's pubs, it's not somewhere you'd find the telly blaring or everyone staring down at their phones. It's a pub for having a chat – be that with a stranger, the bar staff or your friends, the familiar murmur of pub-talk gives the Star a cosy feeling like no other. Traditional Irish music nights are a regular here and the pints, which are possibly the cheapest of any pub in this book, are what you would expect from a pub of this description – smooth, creamy and consistent.

Tyneside Irish Centre

43 Gallowgate, Newcastle upon Tyne, NE1 4SG, England

Newcastle is often thought of as a city that only exists for hen parties and stags. That's not fair, really – they also have decent pints of Guinness. I joke of course, the toon is a city full of life and characters that doesn't take itself too seriously. It's beautiful and the Geordies are some of the friendliest people you will ever meet.

This is the first pub on my list which isn't technically just a pub – it's the Irish centre. With a few thousand members, it is the community hub for the Irish diaspora in Newcastle and hosts social, cultural and educational events. You'd expect a decent pint in that case, and you would be right. It's the perfect place for anyone, Irish or not, to enjoy some Irish music, learn about our culture and sink a couple of lovely pints.

DUBLIN

Ah, Dublin. The rest of Ireland's slightly hated older brother. It is home to some of Ireland's best pubs, filled with history, life and atmosphere, while also home to some of Ireland's worst pubs: tourist traps in Temple Bar designed to drain patrons' wallets while showing them a picture of a leprechaun. But Dublin's beauty still shines through when you know where to go. Hopefully I can help...

The Gravediggers

1 Prospect Square, Glasnevin, Dublin, D09 CF72, Ireland

For me, the Gravediggers in Dublin does the best pint of Guinness in the world, bar none. Founded in 1833, it is a traditional Dublin pub with history at its core, sitting right next to Glasnevin graveyard where Irish greats such as Michael Collins, Constance Markievicz,

Luke Kelly and Brendan Behan are buried. You can pay your respects next door and then settle in. It has sat with the Kavanagh family for generations and is famous for its pint of plain – something that has held true as owner- ship has passed from generation to generation.

A very popular pub, you will often see throngs of people stood outside supping pints, each looking glorious and calling you inside for more. It's very seldom you'd see any pint other than a Guinness being drunk in there – the only other drop you'd regu- larly see would be uisce beatha, the water of life, the perfect chaser to a Guinness that puts fire in the back of your throat and hair on your chest.

The Lord Edward

23 Christchurch Pl, Wood Quay, Dublin, D08 RK00, Ireland

The Lord Edward is a true gem of a pub. Another of Dublin's most famous, it has a beautiful lounge bar, a carpeted floor and circular tables surrounded by circular stools that could keep you talking in circles all night if you gathered the right crowd around them. Inside, you'll find a nice mix of locals, people on the hunt for a great pint of Guinness and the odd American tourist chatting the ear off some poor soul about their great-great-great- grandfather who was born on a farm in County Wicklow. God love them, they're great at talking.

I must admit I was not privy to the joy that was this pub until a couple of years ago, when I visited a friend in Dublin and he introduced me to what would quickly become a pub I miss fondly. A few pints deep, with an Irish tapas board of two flavours of Taytos crisps spread out, the centrepiece of our table, he told me to follow him upstairs for a minute. He took me round the back of the pub and led me up a wooden set of stairs, the walls adorned with some incredible old-school wallpaper that I imagine hasn't been changed for a long, long time. As he approached a set of wooden doors, he put his fingers to his lips, the universal signal to shut up will ya, and barged open the door to reveal a seafood restaurant in full swing, with happy punters everywhere and a beautiful decor. It turns out the Lord Edward has a hugely popular seafood restaurant upstairs that you would absolutely miss

if you weren't privy or paying much attention. While I was downstairs supping pints, lads were upstairs necking bites of seabass and I was none the wiser. For the couple of days in Dublin that followed, I eyed up any pub I entered suspiciously; is there a secret restaurant up there I'm not aware of? Some hidden haddock, some concealed cod?

The Snug Bar

15 Stephen Street Upper, Dublin 8, D08 ADW4, Ireland

The Snug has the cheapest pint in Dublin City that isn't in a pub run by a British man of questionable moral standing that rhymes with leather-moons. That cheap price doesn't indicate a lower quality, no – the pint in the Snug is as good as any in the city, if not better. A local's pub through and through, you get what you get. With one fella serving behind a small bar, there are no frills about this place: no beautiful furniture calls for your bottom, no stunning artistic tapestries adorn its walls. It's a wood-floored, relatively bare pub that does its job and does it well – cheap pints in a great atmosphere with real people. It's the absolute perfect place to be if you're sick of the gentrification of pubs – there has never been a single whisper of a small plate and the only cocktail you're getting is a gin and tonic or a vodka Diet Coke.

The Snug isn't a place I'd heard much of before my first visit – when people speak of the great Dublin pubs, places like the

Palace Bar or Kehoes, it's not often that you'd hear it up there in contention. I actually went in to deliver a T-shirt to the barman. I sell shirts on my website, and with the great postal strike of 2022 coupled alongside Brexit, they've had a bit of a tough time getting from London to the town I know so well. The bartender in there got in touch to say the T-shirt never arrived, so I brought one over when I was on my way to visit a friend in the city and dropped it in. I'd like to pretend that was my sole reason for popping over, a true passion for customer service, but as I was there anyway, it was a great excuse to try a new pub and I'm glad I did. The Snug should absolutely be spoken about in the same vein as Dublin's most iconic pubs.

Fibber Magees

80-81 Parnell St, Rotunda, Dublin 1, D01 CK74, Ireland

I have such a soft spot for Fibbers. A legendary bar with a famous smoking area in a big plaza of sorts that is shared by many other bars and pubs, Fibber's is a spot for rock and metal – a great venue for gigs of that nature. It serves a good pint that can bat with the big hitters, but perhaps gets slightly worse in quality as the bodies pile in and the clock gets closer to striking midnight.

My favourite memory in Fibber's is one of me being extremely, extremely annoying as a teenager. Freshly eighteen, and happy about it after ditching my fake ID (which was just a long-expired passport of a friend who also happened to be blond), we took the classic three-hour Aircoach pilgrimage up to Dublin for a gig. Before the gig, we visited the Temple Bar (the pub, not just the area), a place that inexplicably draws tourists from around Ireland and the world. It might be the worst pub in the world, yet it has a strange draw – people are happy to have spent over a tenner on a pint, twice as much as any other establishment in the city. It's almost a badge of honour to have been scammed there. I think if aliens ever invaded and happened to land in Dublin, they would feel obliged to stop in there to get ripped off before enslaving the earth, just as a courtesy. My go-to advice when someone asks me about their upcoming trip to Dublin is to avoid the Temple Bar, but in my heart I know they're just going to end up there regardless.

Anyway – being eighteen and broke, having a pint in the Temple Bar had decimated our funds for the evening. After the gig, by legendary Australian band Parkway Drive, we headed to Fibber Magee's. On our way, we decided to become the most annoying people in the city, a hard task in Dublin, and try to ask people for cigarettes so we would not need to spend any of our remaining funds on them. After harassing a busload of Japanese tourists, their first experience in Ireland likely being three drunk Cork-men babbling about rollies while making smoking gestures with their hands, we ended up making our way ungracefully through the Fibber's smoking area. I think I ended the night having been given around thirty cigarettes. It's absolutely shameful stuff but ten years on, it makes me laugh more than feel bad about it, and that's all that matters.

The Cappuccino Bar

4-6 Cecilia St, Temple Bar, Dublin, D02 AK29, Ireland

What Irish endeavour would be complete without a bit of nepotism? This country was built on backhanders, brown envelopes, dodgy dealing and slimy men who claim not to have bank accounts. Allow me this one, lads.

My aunt runs the Cappuccino Bar in Dublin – a beautiful spot for a pint, some grub in the mornings, lunchtime or in the evenings and there's no one better to be served by than Maura herself, the queen of good Dublin hospitality.

CORK

Cork people are notorious for believing that Cork is the centre of the universe and the greatest place on earth. I will not say anything to dispel that myth. We are the real capital of Ireland, after all, and some of the best pubs in the world have the pleasure of sitting in Cork.

An Spailpín Fanach

29 S Main St, Centre, Cork, T12 DYX9, Ireland

The Spailpín is one of the best pubs in all of Ireland and a regular haunt of mine any time I return home. It is unique in that it only opens at 7 p.m. – so if I've ever gathered too big a crew on an early sup it is the perfect place to run off to and grab a table when the clock chimes seven. It is an old, traditional Irish pub with fireplaces, incredible snugs where you can hide away with a group of friends to chat, a great pint of Guinness and easy service. They have a traditional Irish music session every Friday night, which is a perfect way to enjoy an evening. There is also a function room upstairs which hosts all manner of events – communist book readings, techno, rap, you name it. The combination in the smoking area of those taking a break from the dance and those stepping out for a cigarette during the trad always makes for an eclectic group of sweaty faces and callused fingers.

The Oval

25 S Main St, Centre, Cork, T12 Y15D, Ireland

The Oval, situated just by the Spailpín, is the pub I will always bring someone to on their first visit to Cork. You enter by opening the front door and pushing through red velvet curtains, revealing a beautiful, dimly lit bar, the air filled with the sounds of rock legends and the quiet hum of chat. There are snugs aplenty throughout the Oval, the perfect nooks to talk away a winter's evening on red leather couches, with the rest of the pub furnished with old wooden tables surrounded by wooden stools.

Standing proud just across the road from the old Beamish & Crawford factory, now defunct, the Oval is famous for having one of the best pints of Beamish (a popular Cork stout), but also serves a beautiful pint of Guinness. There is always a cosy, friendly atmosphere in the pub – it's a breeding ground for smiling faces and soft tones. The staff are some of the most knowledge-able and warm I've ever encountered – whether it's stout, whiskey or ales, they know what direction to point you in.

To me, it is very much a winter pub. The best spot in the pub is situated right at the very back, in a snug with few seats, all facing a roaring fire as if it were

the sun and the chairs were orbiting planets angled towards it for life and sustenance. It is the quintessential spot for a winter's day. Being tucked away in front of that fire with a cold pint in your hand, talking muck to a friend and laughing from the belly is a perfect day to me. No matter where I am in the world, the promise of a pint on a cold winter's day makes me yearn for that spot in the Oval. A frosty boot print on a winter's path, a dusting of ice on a garden wall, smoke billowing from the chimney of a family home – all make me think of the Oval.

Coughlans

7 Douglas St, Ballintemple, Cork, T12 DX39, Ireland

Speaking of Douglas Street, Coughlans is another great spot for a pint of Guinness. It was established in 1831 and is steeped in history, which is very evident from the interior and exterior of the pub. It is a listed building and its famous stone-walled smoking area is as it was when it was built in the 1860s. As well as its pint, it is known for an entertaining night out, often hosting music and comedy gigs in its venue space.

The Laurel

39 Mary Street, Cork, T12 A252, Ireland

The Laurel is a more recent haunt of mine and somewhere I've grown very passionate about over the last year or so. It's a true Cork pub – no frills, no tack, no pandering, just a real pub for real Cork people.

Situated on an unassuming street just beside the river Lee, it would be easy to miss if you weren't looking for it. An unremarkable building with limited signage, it almost looks like just another house along the street – which it still is, in a way. The last time I was there, I saw a lad take the wrong door for the bathroom and end up walking into the living room of the family that owns the place. I like to think that he walked in to find someone with their feet up watching *Deal or No Deal*, but I am not privy to the answer as he left shortly after due to embarrassment.

It is a small pub, with only one person behind the bar at a time, always surrounded by five to seven regulars, high-stool stalwarts who gather to chat an evening away or watch the sport together. There is a dartboard in one corner and rings, a traditional Irish game which involves throwing circular rings onto various hooks on a board and tallying your scores, in another. There are a bunch of screens showing sport throughout and an incredible pool table in the centre. I feel like it's a professional table but I could be wrong. That's what put me on to the pub in the first place – my dad used to drink there in his youth, playing pool with the lads, and I have done my best to follow in his footsteps over the last year or so of visits home.

Charlie's Bar

2 Union Quay, Centre, Cork, T12 XF24, Ireland

Charlie's always reminds me of hard times, which is not a comment on the pub itself at all, but for some reason it is where friends of mine have gathered in times of strife. Breakups, bereavements, misery, we have always ended up there during these times, commiserating with one another and offering support in the way of true Irish men – by solemnly drinking pints together in a dark room and not really mentioning it. We prefer instead to go over memories, like the time I had to chase James, who was shirtless at the time and the hairiest man I've ever met, as he

ran through town crying over his ex in the dead of night at eighteen. Whatever you're going through now can't be worse than that.

Our own personal miseries aside, Charlie's is an excellent pub. It is one of the only famous early houses in Cork City, a place you can drink a pint at 7 a.m. and see all the wonders of the world – late-night workers having a couple before bed and energetic youth still going from the night before. You meet some of the city's most interesting characters sat up in the bar here. It also has a marquee-covered smoking area across the road right next to the river that is nice to sit out in of an evening.

Saying that, my memory of the place is slightly tainted. In summer 2020, during the COVID pandemic, Ireland allowed pubs to serve alcohol, but strictly outside and with table service only. Delighted, and feeling quite pleased with myself after missing home while being in London during lockdown, I decided to get a pint of Guinness and sit down by the river before I went to meet my friends elsewhere. I wanted to look over my city, Cork, which I always miss when I'm gone and where I'm always proud to say I'm from, as I had my first actual draught pint of Guinness for months. Just as I took that first, glorious sup, enjoying the taste of an old friend long missed, one man, sat a few tables down, stood up and projectile vomited over the rail and directly into the river. What's worse is he must have called a round prior to his evacuation, because as he sat down another pint was served to him. The bar staff didn't know that he had just released himself all over the banks of my lovely Lee. Rotten stuff. Mind you, I still finished my pint. Waste not, want not.

Fred Zeppelins

8 Parliament St, Centre, Cork, T12 E299, Ireland

Fred's is Cork's only metal pub and it looks pretty much as you'd imagine. It's so dimly lit that it's hard to know if it's night or day outside. It's quite a small pub, with a slightly tired bar (and vibe) but that's what gives it its glory. It serves a very decent pint of Guinness and has regular metal gigs upstairs that make you feel like the floor is going to cave in underneath you as you dance. The 'smoking area/room' always makes me laugh because it is certainly the most ambiguous smoking area I've ever been to – it's basically just another room but with a slight crack in the ceiling so they can claim that it's open to the outside. It almost feels like the smoking ban never came into effect while you're sat in there.

THE REST OF IRELAND

From north to south and east to west, Ireland is blessed with incredible pubs. Alongside GAA clubs, they are community hubs for villages and towns across the country. I'd love to tour from county to county visiting them all; however I have not been so lucky yet, so here are some of the pubs I have loved from the places I have been.

The Raglan Road

Little Market St, Tramore West, Tramore, Co. Waterford, X91 X795, Ireland

Tired and slightly drunk after an evening with my girlfriend (a Tramore native) and her family, we ducked into the Raglan. It is a traditional Irish pub with stone walls, a low ceiling crossed by wooden beams, an assortment of wooden stools and an impressive collection of whiskeys. There's also a lovely smoking area tucked away upstairs.

Slightly away from the hustle and bustle of the pubs and bars closer to the coastline, the Raglan is a great place to escape for a quiet pint.

Miller's Bar

Tullow Road, Carlow, R93 R2X3, Ireland

One of my favourite memories is from the time when one of my best friends and I used to DJ as a duo called 'Humans of The Sesh', based on a very popular Facebook page we used to run back in 2017 (mentioned earlier in the book) when Facebook was cool and saying 'big bag of cans with the lads' got you eight trillion likes and a booking for Electric Picnic. We were playing in the Foundry nightclub in Carlow, truly one of the most accursed places

I've ever entered, and needed somewhere to have a liquid dinner before our set.

We ended up in Miller's, a pub that has the most perfect two-room set-up – the front bar, in a large room with a ton of seating and always filled with lads, is a great spot for chat, and the backroom contains a free jukebox and a pool table. You can either sit around and chat to the auld fellas in the front, or hop away into the back, play pool and listen to a few choons. It's a bit like a backwards mullet. We opted for the back, and had what I would consider a perfect evening – several pints of beautifully poured Guinness, a few games of pool and then going off to play 'Everytime We Touch' and 'Sandstorm' to a few hundred college students, whether they liked it or not.

Bittle's Bar

70 Upper Church Ln, Belfast, BT1 4QL, Ireland

Bittle's combines my three favourite things beautifully: a creamy pint of Guinness, a drop of whiskey and talking absolute muck. This pub provides all the right conditions to fulfil those needs. The Guinness is incredible, one of the best pints in Ireland, the whiskey selection is extensive and the atmosphere and craic about the place facilitates the talking of muck perfectly.

The bartenders there are proper characters, silver-tongued and happy to take the piss out of you for the slightest slip-up or

hesitation when ordering a pint. You definitely need a thick skin in this place, but the pints well make up for any sort of mick that may get taken out of you while ordering them. They're also known for their tongue-in-cheek signs – the latest one stating that due to Brexit, they can no longer sell half-pints and saying you'll be chucked out the door if you try to smoke a vape inside.

JJ Bowles

8 Thomondgate, Limerick, V94 HK74, Ireland

Limerick has always had an unfairly bad rap in the media. I've always seen it as Cork's upstart younger brother, cheeky and slightly loose. Yeah, it's a little rough around the edges, but so are all of the best pubs. Limerick is excellent. Yurt.

Many of my friends attended the art college there so I spent a lot of time in the city as a young fella, associating it with afters in Park View rather than pristine pints. Saying that, JJ Bowles has always been our spot ever since we grew a fondness for stout and had some money in our back pockets. Sitting next to the river Shannon since 1794, it's Limerick's oldest pub, a beautiful spot that pours an excellent pint, a plaque showing that they were once voted as making 'the best pint of Guinness in Limerick' by the local paper hung proudly on the ancient building's walls. You can appreciate all the elements of nature here – a roaring fireplace can grant you salvation from the cold and the riverside smoking area is a great place to soak up the sun whilst you talk some muck to a stranger.

THE REST OF EUROPE

Drinking pints of Guinness in Europe can be slightly risky. The drink is not quite as popular as it is in Ireland and the UK, so sometimes quality can fall by the wayside. What kind of standards are kept in cities awash with plastic 'Irish' pubs, all named a variation of something like 'Paddy Mac O'Neil O'Shea's' or 'The Wild Rover Michael Collins Eamon DeValera Inn'? I usually avoid them, opting for local spots, but there are times when a nice pint of plain is necessary, and in those moments it's important to know where to find the gold amongst the dirt.

Uisce Beatha

Na vŕšku 341/1, 811 01 Staré Mesto, Slovakia

This is definitely my favourite Irish pub outside of the UK or Ireland. Located down a small alley in Bratislava, and completely missable if you didn't know to look out for it, it's not your typical Irish pub at all. There is one small bar with a couple of tables sitting nearby, and a staircase which leads underground to a little stone-walled cellar filled with wooden tables and chairs, seating maybe twenty people at a push. The Guinness here is delicious and the atmosphere even better.

I visited a few years ago while on my first holiday with my girlfriend and I'm desperate to go back. We had the most incredible evening playing checkers, chess and the other board games they had on offer while drinking Guinness and whiskeys, the type of evening that leads to a drunken kebab and an insatiable desire for McDonalds hash brown the following morning.

Scobie's

Ronda de la Univ., 8, 08007 Barcelona, Spain

I popped into Scobie's for a few the last time I visited Barcelona after hearing whispers of a good pint over the years of running Guinness accounts. I was pleasantly surprised, it tasted just like any regular pint you'd get in London. Solid. It's a great spot for a taste of home when you're abroad. Make sure to enjoy some authentic Irish tapas while you're there – plenty of different flavours of crisps are available.

The Corkonian

Alter Markt 51, 50667 Köln, Germany

The haunt of many a video games journalist and other people in the industry, like myself, this Cork pub serves the best pint of Guinness I've had in Germany. During Gamescom, the biggest gaming convention in the world after the death of E3, this pub becomes a hive of the UK and

Ireland's gaming industry heads. Hang out there after a certain hour and you will hear discussion turn from the previous day's announcements to some of the hardest-hitting NDA-breaking conversations I've ever witnessed. I truly believe the next Elder Scrolls game will one day be leaked via an overheard conversation at the Corkonian at Gamescom – you heard it here first.

Situated along the busy main strip of bars in the city, it's a solid Irish pub with an old wooden lounge-style bar and ample seating inside to watch the match. The pint is decent, but make sure to bring your cash. The bartenders (literally) laugh in the face of those who have yet to understand the penchant for some sweet, sweet coinage.

The Hairy Canary

Archimedesstraat 12, 1000 Brussel, Belgium

Like any other major European city, there is no shortage of Irish pubs in Brussels. On a recent holiday, I was whisked away by another guest from a sophisticated, wine-and-cheese-type dinner with my girl-friend's aunt to attend an FC Irlande party at the Hairy Canary. I was surprised I hadn't heard of the club before – founded in 1989 by Irish players, it has nine teams at different amateur levels. It also throws a great party. The pints in the pub were great and I would definitely recommend it if you have a penchant for a Guinness when visiting the land of chocolate, frites and the European Parliament.

THE REST OF THE WORLD

One of the best parts of being a Guinness drinker is the element of worldwide availability and appeal. It is appreciated all over the world and anyone who is fond of a drop will jump at the opportunity to tell you where to find the best pint. With that, you can pretty safely do a bit of research on the best pints somewhere and end up sitting at a bar on a high stool with a well-poured, creamy pint in your hand. Grand.

Fadó Irish Pub

100 W Grand Ave, Chicago, IL 60654, United States

Lovely pints and great craic. I spent a great couple of nights here on a trip to Chicago a few years back. I was pleasantly surprised by the quality; and it's the perfect place for a bit of grub and a pint of plain. Go visit the big bean, have a drink in the

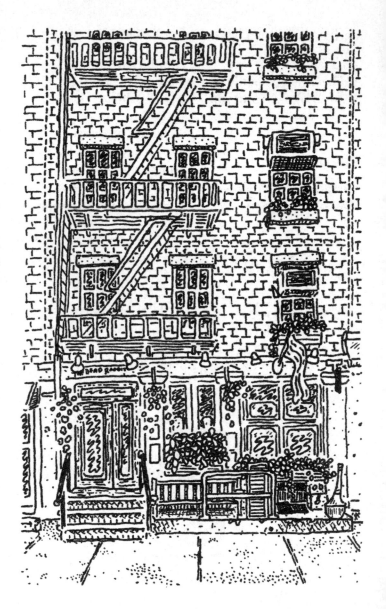

Fadó and see Chicago Fire in an MLS match. As a famous fan once said, come on Seattle (Chicago), fight and win.

The Dead Rabbit

30 Water St, New York, NY 10004, United States

There is no shortage of Irish in New York, a popular destination for us in times of turbulence, and as such, there is certainly no shortage of Irish pubs. The Dead Rabbit is one of the most famous Irish pubs in the world and for good reason – it's great. Tucked away on the Lower East Side of Manhattan, it is renowned for its creamy pints of Guinness and excellent cocktails, each speciality tucked away on separate floors. Downstairs pints, upstairs cocktails. Grand.

The Druid

1357 Cambridge St, Cambridge, MA 02139, United States

Boston is possibly the most Irish city in America. There was a mass migration from Ireland to the city in around 1850, following the Famine, the evidence of which is still apparent to this day – the city is full of Irish pubs and people with Irish heritage, and the Bostonians are mad to chat to anyone with an Irish accent.

The Druid is an Irish-owned Clare pub that serves what I would consider the best Guinness in America. The keg sits directly under the tap, something people claim helps to pour a beautiful pint as the Guinness does not need to travel far through the line to meet the glass. They sell a lot of kegs and the lines are regularly cleaned. There's live Irish music a couple of nights a week and the food is always good – authentic Irish recipes cooked using fresh produce.

The Black Taxi

745-747 N 25th St, Philadelphia, PA 19130, United States

They say it's always sunny in Philadelphia but I'm not really too bothered about the weather – what's the pint situation like? I'm happy to say that it's pretty good and the Black Taxi is the best spot for it. It's your classic American Irish pub – it looks a bit like the ones back home but you have to tip and everyone speaks using their outdoor voice. The stout tap is flowing in there, the telltale sign of a good Guinness to come, and it does not disappoint.

It's a grand aul place to sit down with a massive philly cheesesteak (a beautiful, greasy mess of steak strips, cheese, onion and peppers) and a pint to watch the soccer on the telly. Come on the (Philadelphia) Union. Big man James Connolly would be proud.

The Drunken Poet

65 Peel St, West Melbourne VIC, Australia

Ah, Australia. The home of many an Irishman on the hunt for a different life: more sun, more money, less rain. I feel like the UK and Australia are the two most popular immigrant destinations for us, which makes me wonder whether I may have drawn the short straw. Everyone has a few relatives in Australia – those who set off to 'work for a couple of years and then come back' who have ended up settling down to a lovely life down under. Much like myself, these people miss and want a taste of home. It's not as easy as a cheap Ryanair flight for them, so they seek much-needed reprieve in Irish pubs.

The Drunken Poet is a real Irish pub – small, authentic and cosy, with photos of all of Ireland's greatest people decorating its walls. Whether it's with the owner or the other patrons, it is always a very chatty pub. I wouldn't be afraid to ask the fella sitting next to me at the bar what his thoughts are on Mick McCarthy's 2002 World Cup Irish squad, like.

The Guinness is always flowing and delicious, the best in Melbourne by a country mile.

The Snug Bar

Shop 2 & 3, 752-756, Kingsway, Gymea NSW 2227, Australia

The pint in the Snug is deceptively good. Australia is not known for its top pints of Guinness, yet little nuggets of gold can still be found across the continent. The pub itself does not quite have that generic 'Irish pub' look that you see abroad so often. It doesn't need it. The owners are Irish and they pour an excellent pint of Guinness – that's all you need to get my seal of approval, at least. With such a welcoming atmosphere, it certainly feels like a little piece of home away from home.

Conclusion

Well, that's it. The end of a book is a bit like the end of the night in a pub, but I won't do the Irish goodbye of which I am so fond to you readers. I only do it usually because everyone I start to say goodbye to ends up asking me to stay for another and my well-intentioned departure will inevitably end up with me staying and singing 'The Irish Rover' with a gang of lads as the pub begins to close. You, the reader, cannot ask me to stay on, so I'm fairly safe to say my goodbyes this time around.

We've covered a lot in this book. We looked at the history of Guinness and how it became the globally recognised brand it is today, why some pints are good and some are bad, and some of the best pubs from around the world to get a pint of plain in. We've also talked about my friend James's hairy chest, a vampire Elvis impersonator and even John Cena trading cards, so we've done well in my opinion.

The most important thing I'd like readers to take away is that while it's great to get a lovely pint of

Guinness, it's the atmosphere and the company that you drink it in that makes it special. There is no point in drinking the most pristine, accurate-to-the-measure, perfect pint of Guinness in a dull, lifeless, blank-walled box. The beauty of the pint lies in where you enjoy it and the people you enjoy it with. It's the characters you meet, the stories you'll still tell in ten years' time, the kind landlord you chatted to for half an hour on a cold winter afternoon when you needed cheering up. For me, that's what it's all about.

I'll see ye up at the bar, so. Sláinte.

END

The man, the myth, the legend

Ian Ryan is a London-based Corkman, doggedly pursuing a decent pint in the capital since 2018. He has made a name for himself as the founder of popular social media accounts Shit London Guinness and Beautiful Pints. His expertise comes from many a drink sank and enjoyed. When not posting plain across Instagram and Twitter, Ryan spends his days in the world of video games (working, not just playing).